THE LADDER TO SUCCESS

Steps to Achieving Leadership, Loving Relationships, Financial Security, Health, and True Happiness

ABOUT OUR ORGANIZATION

Ladder to Success, Inc.
www.laddertosuccess.com
theladdertosuccess@finding-freedom.com
1-801-755-5323

Ladder to Success's mission is to help individuals, families, businesses and organizations learn and live the principles of success. This mission is achieved through:

Business Opportunities

Ladder to Success provides the world's greatest business opportunity. If you can find a better business opportunity, Ladder to Success will give you $1000. We help individuals and families begin their own business providing them with the resources, systems, and training they need to succeed. We have helped thousands of people achieve financial freedom, and we can do the same for you. For more information about this opportunity, call 1-801-755-5323.

Books

We have read and researched thousands of books to assemble a core of books that best facilitate the learning and living of the principles of success.

Articles

We have also built a library of articles to help people learn and live the principles of success.

Lectures

We will gladly come and speak at businesses, churches, and schools. We have developed a series of lectures. You can request such topics as Christlike Leadership, Vision, Excellence, Integrity, Living a Balanced Life, Relationships, Communication, Leadership Styles, The Four Ways to Create Wealth, and many more. We can also develop a presentation tailored to your needs and desires. To schedule a lecture, call 1-801-755-5323.

Audio Tapes

How do you spend time in your car? Why not utilize driving time learning the principles that will bring success in every facet of your life? We have assembled a number of audio tapes which teach the principles of success. This book, *The Ladder to Success*, is also available on audio tape. It can be purchased by calling 1-801-755-5323.

Statement of Excellence Workshop

We believe that one of the most powerful ways to obtain excellence and success in every aspect of your life is by developing a personal Statement of Excellence. A Statement of Excellence includes a dream statement, mission statement, values statement, and long-term goals. Developing a Statement of Excellence will be the best decision you will ever make. Ladder to Success has developed a book designed to take you step by step through this process. This book can be ordered by calling 1-801-755-5323.

Courses

Many organizations already have implemented courses around the book *The Ladder to Success*. We are in the process of developing courses which can be taught in Seminaries, Institutes, Schools, Churches, Businesses, and other Organizations. Contact us for further information on these courses.

Published by
Platinum Publishing
Salt Lake City, UT

Printed in the United States of America

Dedicated to our parents—Wayne and Nadine Taylor and Curtis and Virginia Ledbetter.

ACKNOWLEDGMENTS

We would like to express thanks to the many people who helped, directly and indirectly, with the compilation of this work. We would like to express thanks:

Lennon's

- To my beautiful bride Suzanne for her sincere Christlike love and for her loyalty to me and our children.
- To Sky for his obedience and for his desire to achieve his personal best.
- To Brittany for the great love she shows to me and our family.
- To Holly for her excitement, energy, smile and love of life.
- To Leah for the happiness and light she brings into our home.
- To my business partners for teaching me that individuals grow but teams explode.
- To my parents, Curtis and Virginia, for all they have taught me.
- To my brother, Rob, and his wife, Katie, for being great business partners.
- To Lynda and Lane for being great sisters.

Cameron's

- To God for the plan of salvation and His vision. To Jesus Christ for providing life and giving us a perfect model of leadership to pattern our lives after. The Holy Ghost for reminding me of what is truly important and for providing inspiration. I recognize that I am nothing without God and anything that I have achieved or will achieve is a result of Him. I can take no credit for any of this work. If a home run is hit, does the crowd honor the bat which actually made contact with the ball and hit it out of the park? Of course not, but often in our lives we take credit for our accomplishments or honor others for their accomplishments with little or no credit given to God. All glory and credit must go to God. Taking any credit for this work would be as foolish as me giving praise to a bat for hitting a home run.
- To Shauna Barrett. She completed some of the research for the project and provided me with insights and ideas that have vastly improved the quality of this work. She is truly one of a kind – amazing. I thoroughly enjoyed working with her. She also helped me outside of work by being an example and a great friend.
- To Jesse Todd. His encouragement and belief in me increased my drive to succeed and complete a book that would inspire and help others. I spent

many hours talking to him about leadership development. Many of the ideas in the book stem from the learning we did together.

- To Paula Brackett for her love of people and Christlike leadership.

- To the BYU Student Leadership Seminar for their commitment to and development of Christlike leadership materials.

- To Jon Hyatt. Jon does outstanding work. He is an example of excellence. Sometimes I thought he should be the one writing this book. He helped me to get done the things that needed to be done, allowing me more time to focus on this work.

- To Rob Reinhart, Adam Koch, Sam McGuire, Liz and Ryan Evans, Dave, Mark Archibold, Tom and Rachel Orem, Ben and Kim Candleland, Lindsey Welch, Joel Barrett, Lori Mauher, Danae and Lindsey Wall, Nicole, Steve and Lori, Jen, Aaron, Brooke, and Nathan Burningham, Heinz Kirchhausen, Harmony and Ashley Lethcoe, Tracey Mower, Barnaby Vergara, Tim Olsen, Tyrus Papa, Glenn Hatfield, Jason Hymus, Elizabeth Palmer, Shannon Jensen, Amber Poole, Jamie Coon, and Dan McNeff for being such wonderful friends.

- To Myra Carlsruh for being a good friend and for helping with the editing.

- To Sandra Holman for helping with the editing and proofreading.

- To Michael McCleve for his support and counsel.

- To Brady and Amy Taylor. To Brady for his continual kindness and example and for being such a great golfing partner. To Amy for helping with the editing. Her talents as a writer and editor greatly improved the quality of this work. She did things that my associates and I could not do and for that I am extremely grateful.

- To my Mom and Dad, Wayne and Nadine Taylor. The service they have provided has made many of my opportunities in life possible.

- To Koby, Spencer, Tyson, and Debra for being great siblings and for never doubting my dreams.

- To Lennon Ledbetter, Brad Hardisty, Dave Tidwell, and Steve, Cecile and Helen Thomas, for helping me build a successful business and find financial freedom.

CONTENTS

PREFACE by Cameron

The principles of success and the principles of Divine-Centered Leadership are one in the same. This book is designed to help people learn and live the principles of success such as goal setting, vision, taking the initiative, managing conflict, integrity, relationships, communication, service, and delegation.

Throughout my years of education in grade school, high school, public colleges, and private universities, I have always felt like there was something missing. That there were things I needed to know to be successful which were not being taught and emphasized.

During my years of study at a nationally recognized private university, I recall recruiters coming into my various classes to tell us what they were looking for in their employees. The recruiters would say they wanted people who were easy to get along with and good with people, people who were honest, people who were good listeners, people who were leaders and self starters, people who had goals and direction in their lives, people driven to excel.

I recall attending lectures of successful employees and entrepreneurs who had graduated from the university and achieved great success returning to give their advice about how to succeed. They would make suggestions such as set clear long-term and short-term goals, learn how to communicate and get along with people, and learn how to live a balanced life. Never did any of them recommend taking more math classes or getting higher test scores. They all emphasized learning the principles of success because they are the key to achievement and a wonderful life.

Teddy Roosevelt said, "The most important single ingredient to the formula of success is knowing how to get along with people."

I wanted to succeed in life so I began to seek ways to learn and live the principles those who had achieved success where recommending. I began to analyze the curriculum of the courses I was required to study throughout my life to see how much I was learning about the principles of success. It was amazing to me how little grade schools, high schools, and universities focus on the principles of success.

The education I received was excellent and beneficial but it was far from complete. Although I graduated from high school as a salutatorian and attended several universities graduating with honors, I learned little about goal setting, listening, vision, integrity, managing conflict, building relationships, getting along with people, leadership, and delegation. The principles of success simply are not a part of most education systems curriculum. The key to financial security, to loving relationships with family and friends, to success in the workplace, to achieving leadership, to health, and true happiness is learning and living in accordance with the principles of success. The truth is that most people, even those with college degrees, have learned little about the principles of success.

So, if we do not learn the principles of success in school, where do we learn them? This book was written to help people learn and live in accordance with the principles of success so they can live the full, happy, productive life God intended them to live.

PART I

There is a Need

STEP 3: ***Showing the Way***
Leading Others to Success

STEP 2: ***Going the Way***
Leading by Example, Being a Person of Intergrity

STEP 1: ***Knowing the Way***
Having Vison, Providing Direction and Purpose

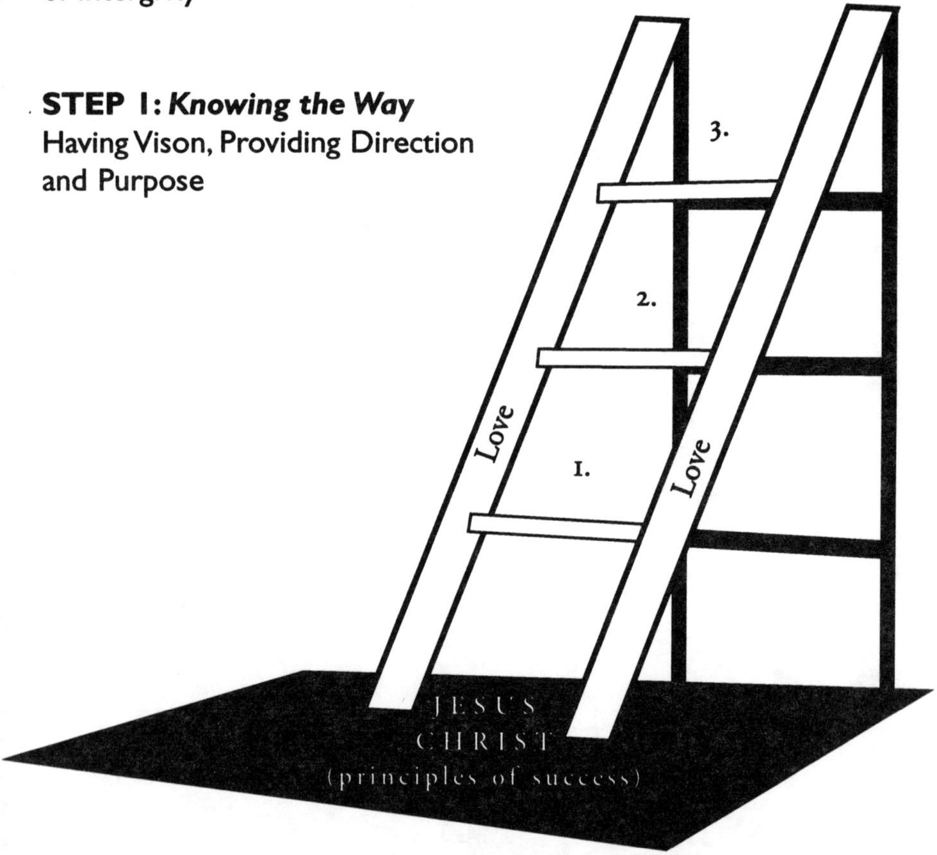

"It is upon the rock of our Redeemer who is Christ the Son of God that ye must build your foundation."

PART 1: INTRODUCTION: THERE IS A NEED

It is our hope and desire that you will take the time and effort necessary to learn and apply the material contained in this book. The benefits of leadership that follow are presented to help you understand the great importance of leadership and its benefits.

Why Should You Learn About Divine-Centered Leadership (The Principles of Success)? Because . . .

1. There is a Need for Christlike Leadership in the Home.

Success comes from focusing on the root or source of problems. However, we often spend time addressing and solving problems of lesser importance—problems which are a result of a core problem. As Henry David Thoreau said, "For every thousand hacking at the leaves of evil, there is one striking at the root." As we identify and address root and core problems, we will make true progress. As we solve core problems, many other problems will disappear. As we do an analysis on many problems in the world, we find they stem back to the family. The root is the family and leadership in the family.

Today there is a leadership crisis in the home. For example, over the past 30 years the percentage of families headed by a single parent has more than tripled. The divorce rate has more than doubled, and currently the average child spends seven hours a day watching TV and five minutes a day with dad.

Also over the past 30 years:

- Teenage suicide has increased almost 300 percent.
- Scholastic Aptitude Test scores among all students have dropped 73 points.
- Juvenile Violent Crime has increased 500 percent
- Since 1940 the top disciplinary problems in public school have changed from chewing gum and running in the halls to teen pregnancy, rape, drug abuse, and assault.

There is a leadership crisis in the home. More than ever before there is a need for family leadership. The family is the foundation of society. It is the building block of every nation. It is the glue by which everything is held together. Whether we succeed or fail as a people depends on our effectiveness as parents. We must understand that, more than at any other time in history, the role of parenting is absolutely vital and irreplaceable. Having and raising a family is the most important thing any of us will ever do.

To succeed as a parents requires more than good ideas and a desire to create a strong family. It requires a set of skills. Creating an effective family requires numerous attributes, skills, and abilities. More skills are needed to effectively run a family than to be a successful business man, dentist, engineer, or doctor.

We know that becoming a dentist, business man, or engineer takes thousands of hours of study and practice. We spend the time and money needed to learn a profession, but many spend little time and money learning to be an effective parent. There is a mentality that learning to be a parent is just something that happens.

Many people are trustworthy in terms of character. Their desires are good, but they are simply not competent—they lack the knowledge and skills needed to be a successful parent. Becoming a successful parent is not just something that happens it is something that requires extensive study, personal development, and work.

No one would ever say "I was a born engineer" or "I'm a dentist—it was just something that kinda happened." But for years that has been the attitude of many toward parenting. We can become parents by simply having sex. However, to become an effective parent requires much more. A parent is ultimately a leader. I cannot think of a better illustration of a leader than that of a parent. To become an effective leader and parent it takes thousands of hours of study and practice just as it takes thousands of hours to become a good doctor, teacher, or engineer. Leadership can be taught and it can be mastered, as can any profession. Our success as parents depends on us developing the attributes and learning the skills of an effective leader.

We spend thousands of hours and years of our life studying in school to become teachers, engineers, or whatever other profession we have chosen. However, how much time do we spend developing the leadership ability needed to be an effective parent? How much time do we spend learning to succeed in the most important stewardship we will ever have—that of parents? Now is the time to prepare ourselves to fulfill our stewardship as fathers and mothers. Does a dentist wait until he has an office and patients to begin learning how to be a dentist—just doing what he remembers his dentist doing and learning by trial and error along the way? Absolutely not. Have you ever heard anyone say, "Man, I would like to build an hydroelectric damn across that river. I will just start building and kinda learn as I go?" Of course not.

We can summarize our comments into three categories: what, why, and how. The "what" is that the most important stewardship we will ever possess is that of parents. We have a responsibility to develop the skills needed to successfully fulfill that stewardship. "Why?" Because whether we succeed or fail as a people depends on our effectiveness as parents, and all who fail to fulfill family responsibilities will one day stand accountable before God. And "how" do we prepare ourselves to become parents—by studying and developing Divine-Centered Leadership abilities.

Christ is our ultimate resource for successful parenting. Christ is the foundation upon which if man will build they shall never fall. "If we want to be successful, He is our pattern. All the ennobling, perfect, and beautiful qualities of maturity, of strength, and of courage are found in the Master Jesus Christ."[1]

2. Leadership=Success

The principles of Divine-Centered Leadership will make you more successful in your personal, social, financial, and spiritual lives. The principles of Divine-Centered Leadership and the principles of success are one in the same.

"Everything rises and falls on leadership...The effectiveness of your work will never rise above your ability to lead and influence others. You cannot produce consistently on a level higher than your leadership. In other words, your leadership skills determine the level of your success—and the success of those who work around you."[2]

3. You are a Leader

"Everyone is a leader or has influence in the lives of others even though he may not realize it. The question is: What kind of leader will he be? What kind of influence will he have? Each individual must make his own decision as to what kind he will be. He should be determined to be the kind who can say as Jesus said, 'Come follow me and do as ye see me do,' knowing that he is leading in the path of truth and righteousness. This should be the aim of every leader."[3]

"Every individual, regardless of position or station in life, is a leader. Not merely having the potential to lead, but is, in fact, a leader. At the very least, the individual is a leader of one—himself. For no one can give away the responsibility of leading his own life; this can only be done by the bearer of that life." (Michael McCleve)

4. There is a Need for Leaders

The world is in need of leaders. General Mark W. Clark, a WWII officer, said, "All nations seek it constantly, because it is the key to greatness, sometimes to surviva…the electric and the elusive quality known as leadership. Where does juvenile delinquency begin? In leaderless families. Where do slums fester? In leaderless cities. Which armies falter, which political parties fail? Poorly led ones. Contrary to the old saying that leaders are born not made, the art of leading can be taught and it can be mastered."[4]

5. Leadership Enables You to Cultivate Better Relationships

What things are most important to you? Chances are, most things of importance to you involve people and relationships. While most people state that relationships rank most important in their lives, they spend little time developing their ability to form and sustain meaningful relationships. If someone desires to be a dentist or engineer, he or she will spend years developing the abilities to be successful. Do you want to have meaningful relationships and be a positive influence on those around you? Then you must spend the time developing your abilities. And the ability to develop relationships and impact others for good is learned through the study of Divine-Centered Leadership.

6. Leadership Will Help You Reach Your Full Potential

Most people perform far below their capabilities. What is your potential? What is the potential of those around you? Leadership enables you to reach your full potential and help others perform at theirs. Within each of us there is a vast reservoir of abilities that are dormant. Studying leadership will enable you to discover and tap those reservoirs inside yourself and others.

7. Leadership Results in Financial Blessings

Studies reveal that the principles of leadership contribute the greatest to job success. "These investigations revealed that even in such technical lines as engineering, about 15 percent of one's financial success is due to one's technical knowledge and about 85 percent is due to skill in human engineering—to personality and the ability to lead people." Therefore, if you desire to increase your marketability, you should develop leadership attributes and skills. "One can, for example, hire mere technical ability in engineering, accountancy, architecture or any other profession at nominal salaries. But the person who has technical knowledge plus the ability to express ideas, to assume leadership, and to arouse enthusiasm among people—that person is headed for higher earning power. In the heyday of his activity, John D. Rockefeller said that 'the ability to deal with people is as purchasable a commodity as sugar or coffee. And I will pay more for that ability,' said John D., 'than for any other under the sun.'"[5]

Since leadership is a quality worth more than anything "under the sun," you would think that every university would make it a vital part of their curriculum, but the truth is that during a four-year university experience students learn little about leadership. Since universities spend little time developing students' leadership abilities, the smart student will recognize the benefits of leadership and spend the time necessary to develop these abilities—to learn the principles of success.

Divine-Centered Leaders never seek money for selfish reasons. Divine-Centered Leaders seek first to do God's will. They seek to serve. Divine-Centered Leaders live in accordance with the commandments found in Matthew 6:33 and Jacob 2:19. "Seek ye first the kingdom of God, and his righteousness; and all these things shall be added unto you." "And after ye have obtained a hope in Christ ye shall obtain riches, if ye seek them; and will seek them for the intent to do good—to cloth the naked, and to feed the hungry, and to liberate the captive, and administer relief to the sick and the afflicted."

Money is a desirable object. Money enables us to provide for our families. Money enables us to help the unfortunate. Money gives us the freedom to do the things that are truly important. Money enables us to spend time with our children. Money enables one to live life to its full potential. "What's puzzling about money is the backward approach so many people use in trying to make it. Everywhere you see people with a 'money first' attitude. Yet these same people always have little money. Why? Simply this: that they forget money can't be harvested unless they plant the seeds that grow money. And the seed of money is service. That's why 'put-service-first' is an attitude which creates wealth. Put service first and money will take care of itself."[6]

If you serve others, you will be blessed financially. Service is the seed that brings forth the fruit of wealth. Money is not good or bad. Good people with money do good things with their money, and bad people with money do bad things with it.

8. You Will Become More Like Jesus Christ.

The purpose of Divine-Centered Leadership is to facilitate the development of Christlike leaders—to help others lead as Christ led. In order to lead as Christ lead, you must become like He is. The study of Divine-Centered Leadership will help you develop into a more Christlike person.

9. The Principles of Success Increase Productivity

Learning and living the principles of success can be compared to a skilled craftsman acquiring tools to make himself more productive. A farmer with only a shovel can do a certain level of production. Give that same farmer a tractor and how much more can that same farmer produce? In 1930, there were 30 million farmers in the U.S. and they fed about 100 million citizens. Today there are fewer than 300,000 farmers producing food to feed 270 million Americans plus another 100 million throughout the rest of the world. In only 70 years, improved tools have enabled one percent of the farmers to produce more than four times as much food.

Take another example—transportation. It takes a tool to get us where we want to go. Over the years, we have moved from the horse and buggy to trains, cars, and airplanes. Each new tool has enabled us to reach our destination in a shorter period of time. In the 1800's it took the pioneers years to cross the plains to the west. Today, with improved tools, we can make the same journey in a few hours.

As people learn and live the principles of success, we will see a great increase in the productivity of people. Just as one percent of the farmers can produce four times as much food with improved tools as the farmer 70 years ago, so will those who learn and live the principles of success greatly increase their productivity and success.

PART 2

The Ladder Model of Divine-Centered Leadership

STEP 3: ***Showing the Way***
Leading Others to Success

STEP 2: ***Going the Way***
Leading by Example, Being a Person of Intergrity

STEP 1: ***Knowing the Way***
Having Vison, Providing Direction and Purpose

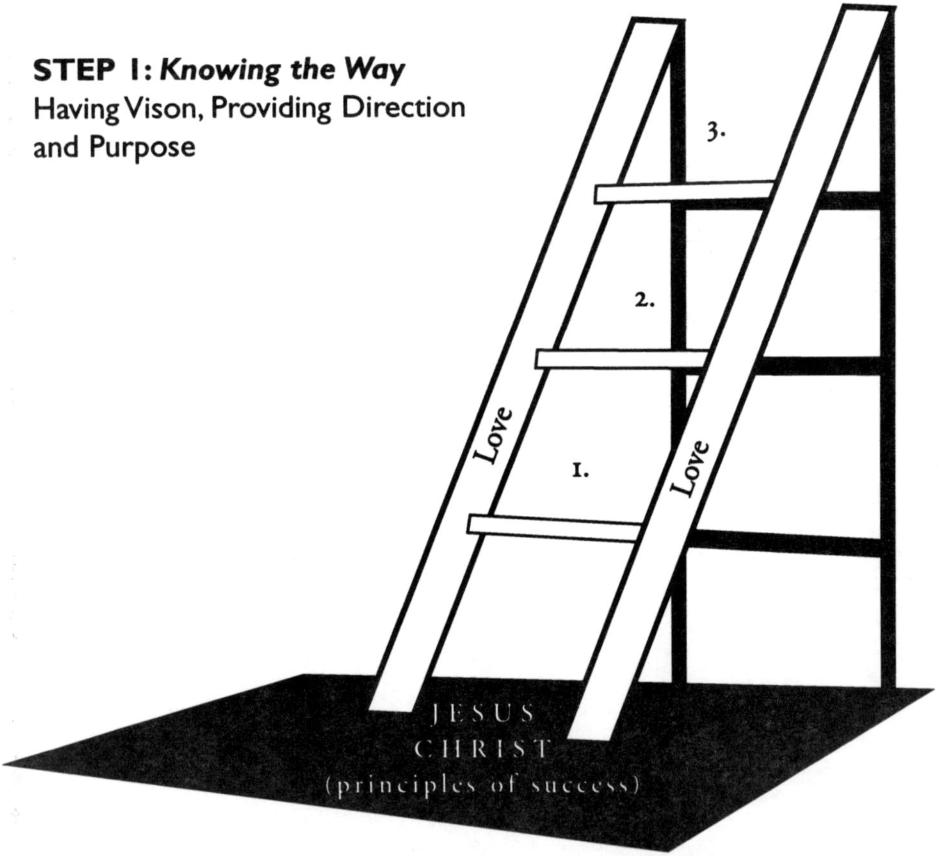

"It is upon the rock of our Redeemer who is Christ the Son of God that ye must build your foundation."

PART 2: THE LADDER MODEL OF DIVINE-CENTERED LEADERSHIP

Many have recognized the importance and effectiveness of Jesus' words and methods of leadership. However, several people have told us that we shouldn't try to define leadership or put how Christ leads into a model—that learning leadership is an endeavor you learn by living which doesn't need models, neat little dogmas and formulas. We find their argument somewhat foolish, and we have rejected their advice. We believe that anyone who wants to learn Christlike leadership would like to have the clearest and most accurate ideas about Christ's leadership which are available. We admit the model is not perfect or complete, just as a map of the earth does not contain every aspect of the continents, islands, and oceans and doesn't present them perfectly, but a map of the earth does depict our best understanding of the continents, islands, and oceans.

"The map is admittedly only colored paper, but there are two things you have to remember about it. In the first place, it is based on what hundreds and thousands of people have found out by sailing the real Atlantic. In that way it has behind it masses of experience just as real as the one you could have from the beach; only, while yours would be a single isolated glimpse, the map fits all those different experiences together. In the second place, if you want to go anywhere, the map is absolutely necessary. As long as you are content with walks on the beach, your own glimpses are far more fun than looking at a map. But the map is going to be more use than walks on the beach if you want to go to America."[1]

This book organizes Jesus Christ's ideas and methods of leadership into a ladder model with the Master Jesus Christ as the foundation, love as the parallel side pieces, and Knowing the Way, Going the Way, and Showing the Way as the three rungs.

The ladder model of Divine-Centered Leadership is the clearest depiction available on how a Christlike person leads. If you want to become a Christlike leader, a map on how to become such is essential. How effective is it to try to travel someplace without some kind of a map? The ladder model serves as a map to help people become

Christlike leaders. A map is essential but it also must be applied to be of benefit. Just as you can't simply look at a map and expect to get anywhere, so must the ideas in the ladder model be applied.

We will begin by discussing each part of the ladder model.

Jesus Christ: The Foundation of Divine-Centered Leadership

Jesus Christ is the foundation of Divine-Centered Leadership. "If we would be eminently successful, He is our pattern. All the ennobling, perfect, and beautiful qualities of maturity, of strength, and of courage are found in Jesus Christ."[2]

"Every person builds a house of faith. We do so either knowingly or unknowingly. And every builder soon learns that a good building with a bad foundation is worse than useless; it is dangerous. As one Christian writer has observed: 'If the stability of buildings depends largely on their foundations, so does the stability of human lives. The search for personal security is a primal instinct, but many fail to find it today. Old familiar landmarks are being obliterated. Moral absolutes which were once thought to be eternal are being abandoned.'[3] Thus, our house of faith can be no more secure than the foundation upon which it is built. Foolish men build upon the shifting sands of ethics and the marshlands of human philosophies and doctrines. The wise build upon the rock of revelation, heeding carefully the living oracles, lest they be 'brought under condemnation…and stumble and fall when the storms descend… And beat upon their house'[4]"[5]

When we base our leadership development on Christ's teachings and example, we can know that we are building upon a solid foundation. Christ is our source of truth and our model of effective leadership.

We will become successful as we turn our lives over to Christ. He is our source of greatness. Once we realize our own nothingness and our reliance on Christ, we can truly become great. Once we forget our will and desires and submit to the will and desires of the Lord, we will have true success. As C. S. Lewis taught, "Give up yourself, and you will find your real self. Lose your life and you will save it. Submit to death, death of your ambitions and favorite wishes every day and death of your whole body in the end: submit with every fibre of your being, and you will find eternal life. Keep back nothing. Nothing that you have not given away will ever be really yours. Nothing in you that has not died will ever be raised from the dead. Look for yourself, and you will find in the long run only hatred, loneliness, despair, rage, ruin, and decay. But look for Christ and you will find Him, and with Him everything else thrown in."[6]

You may now ask, if we all are doing the will of God, are we all not exactly the same? No. Actually, coming to Christ and turning our life over to him cultivates diversity. As we come to Christ, we find our true selves. We come to see how different we truly are. Let's take power tools for example. There are all kinds of power tools—drills, sanders, saws, etc. They are all tools, but each is very different. The difference between these tools is manifest when they are plugged into an outlet—the tools' power source. When the tools are operating on electricity, they demonstrate how different they are. The sander smooths objects, the drill produces holes, and the saw cuts. Each is operating on the same power source but each is very different. When you take away the power source—electricity—they become very much the same. They all become as paper weights. Our power source is Christ. Until we submit our will to His we will never find our true selves. "He that findeth his life shall lose it: and he that loseth his life for my sake shall find it." (Matthew 10:39)

Love: The "Sine Qua Non" of Divine-Centered Leadership

"Sine Qua Non" is a Latin phrase meaning "without which not." If love is not present, leadership will not occur. An atmosphere of love must exist for one person to influence another for good. "When we truly love others without condition, without strings, we help them feel secure and safe and validated and affirmed in their essential worth, identity, and integrity. Their natural growth process is encouraged. We make it easier for them to live the laws of life—cooperation, contribution, self-discipline, integrity—and to discover and live true to the highest and best within them."[7]

There is nothing more powerful than the principle of unconditional love when influencing others for good. As taught a religious leader, "Nothing is so much calculated to lead people to forsake sin as to take them by the hand, and watch over them with tenderness. When persons manifest the least kindness and love to me, O what power it has over my mind, while the opposite course has a tendency to harrow up all the harsh feelings and depress the human mind."[8]

The following story, shared by Howard W. Hunter illustrates well the powerful influence of love:

"After his father became ill, Vern Crowley took responsibility for running the family wrecking yard although he was only fifteen years of age. Some customers occasionally took unfair advantage of the young man, and parts were disappearing from the lot overnight. Vern was angry and vowed to catch someone and make an example out of him. Vengeance would be his.

Just after his father had started to recover from his illness, Vern was making his rounds of the yard one night at closing time. It was nearly dark. In the distant corner of the property, he caught sight of someone carrying a large piece of machinery toward the back fence. He ran like a champion athlete and caught the young thief. His first thought was to take out his frustrations with his fists and then drag the boy to the front office and call the police. His heart was full of anger and vengeance. He had caught his thief, and he intended to get his just dues.

Out of nowhere Vern's father came along, put his weak and infirm hand on his son's shoulder, and said, "I see you're a bit upset, Vern. Can I handle this?" He then walked over to the young would-be thief and put his arm around his shoulder, looked him in the eye for a moment, and said, "Son, tell me, why are you doing this? Why were you trying to steal the transmission?" Then Mr. Crowley started walking toward the office with his arm around the boy, asking questions about the young man's car problems as they walked. By the time they had arrived at the office, the father said, "Well, I think your clutch is gone and that's causing your problem."

In the meantime, Vern was fuming. "Who cares about the clutch?" he thought. "Let's call the police and get this over with." But his father just kept talking. "Vern, get him a clutch. Get him a throw out bearing, too. And get him a pressure plate. That should take care of it." The father handed all of the parts to the young man. "Just ask for it. There is a way out of every problem. People are willing to help."

Vern Crowley said he learned an everlasting lesson in love that day. The young man came back to the lot often. Voluntarily, month by month, he paid for all the parts Vic Crowley had given him, including the transmission. During those visits, he asked Vern why his dad was the way he was and why he did what he did. Vern told him something of their [Christian] beliefs and how much his father loved the Lord and loved people. Eventually the would-be thief was baptized. Vern later said, "It's hard now to describe the feelings I had and what I went through in that experience. I, too, was young. I had caught my crook. I was going to extract the utmost penalty. But my father taught me a different way." A different way? A better way? Oh, how the world could benefit from such a magnificent lesson."[9]

Not only is love the most effective method of influence, it is the only method approved by the Lord. "No power or influence can or ought to be maintained by virtue of the priesthood, only by persuasion, by long-suffering, by gentleness and meekness, and by love unfeigned."[10] Divine-Centered Leaders are full of love and lead others because they love them. Love creates an environment where Divine-Centered Leadership can flourish. Love is the great facilitator of leadership—the "sine qua non."

Knowing the Way, Going the Way, Showing the Way

Divine-Centered Leadership is a process, not the result of a position. Leadership is a three-fold process of Knowing the Way, Going the Way, and Showing the Way. What does it mean to know, go and show the way?

Step 1. *Knowing the Way*—having vision, providing direction and purpose.
Step 2. *Going the Way*—leading by example, being a person of integrity.
Step 3. *Showing the Way*—leading others to success.

"Knowing the Way" is the first step to leadership because you must know what it is you are leading people to. Leaders are pioneers. Leaders take people places. However, we can't lead until we have somewhere to go. We've all heard the familiar saying "a journey of a thousand miles begins with a single step," but a journey of a thousand miles is pointless unless we know where we are going and why we want to get there. Divine-Centered Leaders know where they are going. They have vision, and their vision is inspired. However, only "Knowing the Way" does not make a leader. A leader must also lead by example. People who have vision but no action are dreamers, not leaders. In addition to "Knowing the Way," a leader must "Go the Way."

The second step of leadership (Going the Way) is one of personal development: learning, doing, and becoming. The process of personal development places people in a position to help others. Harold B. Lee said, "You cannot lift another soul until you are standing on higher ground than he is." Personal success precedes success with others. As the Savior taught in Matthew 7:3-5, "And why beholdest thou the mote that is in thy brother's eye, but considerest not the beam that is in thine own eye? Or how wilt thou say to thy brother, let me pull out the mote out of thine eye; and behold, a beam is in thine own eye? Thou hypocrite, first cast out the beam out of thine own eye, and then shalt thou see clearly to cast out the mote out of thy brother's eye." However, it is possible to obtain personal success without being a leader. For leaders are not defined by their personal success but by the accomplishments of their followers. Once we "Know the Way" and are "Going the Way," we are in a position to "Show the Way" to others.

"Showing the Way" is where the change and growth of others takes place. Let's say you are great at the elements classified as "Knowing the Way" and "Going the Way," yet fail at the elements of "Showing the Way" to others. Are you a leader? No. In addition to effectively setting vision and purpose and obtaining personal successes, leaders must enable their followers to obtain goals. People may be successful, but they are not leaders until they make others successful as well.

All three steps (Knowing, Going and Showing) must be completed for leadership to occur.

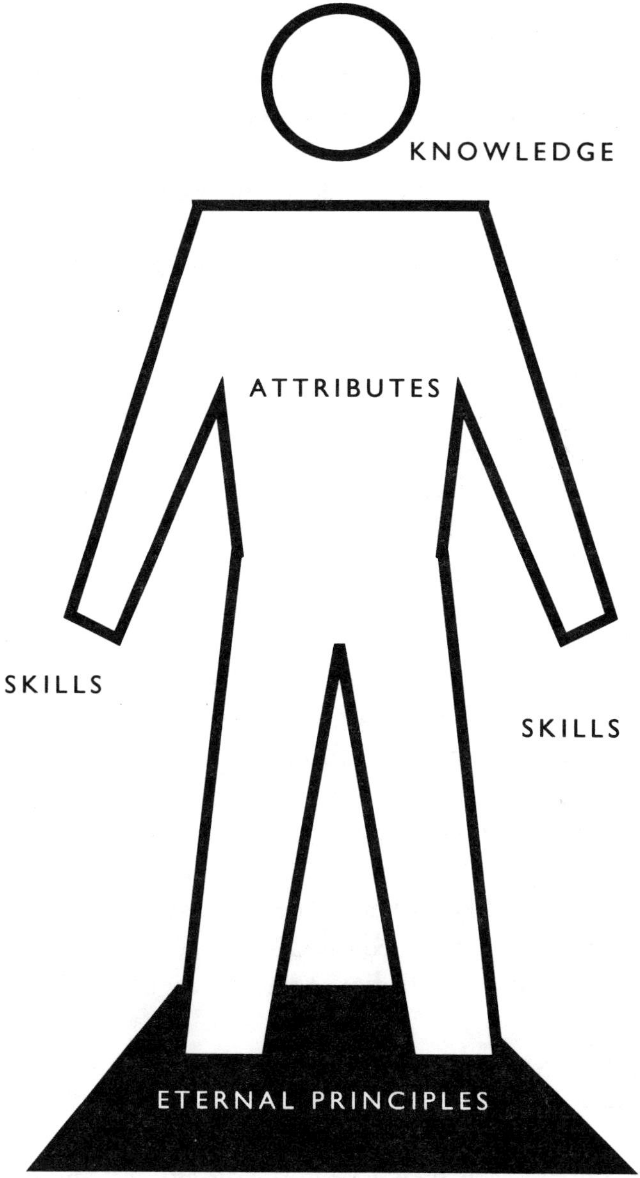

Elements of an Effective Leader

Elements of Effective Leaders

There are key components of leadership we must possess to Know, Go and Show the Way. Leadership elements can be broken into four main categories: living in accordance with Eternal principles, knowledge, skills, and attributes. A leader must be developed in each area to be successful. The four elements are interrelated, but we will begin by addressing each element separately.

Living in Accordance with Eternal Principles: A Key Element of Effective Leaders

"Whosoever will keep the commandments of God, . . . will rise and not fall, they will lead and not follow, they will go upward and not downward. God will exalt them and magnify them before the nations of the earth, and he will set the seal of his approval upon them, will name them as his own. This is my testimony to you."

—Joseph F. Smith

Just as the earth is governed by certain generalities called the laws of nature such as gravity, so are men governed by laws called Eternal principles such as honesty and justice.

Just as events in the physical universe have natural causes which always precede them in time, which can be explained rationally in terms of the laws of nature, so can events in human life be predicted and explained in terms of Eternal principles. "There is a law, irrevocably decreed in heaven before the foundation of this world, upon which all blessings are predicated—And when we obtain any blessing from God, it is by obedience to that law upon which it is predicated."[11]

Just as the laws of nature are the same everywhere in the universe, Eternal principles are the same for all people.

The laws of nature have remained the same throughout time. They are the same now as they were in the distant past and will be in the future. Eternal Principles have been and will be the same forever.

The laws of nature and Eternal principles have many similar characteristics; however, there is one great difference. We cannot disobey the laws of nature such as gravity, but we can disobey Eternal principles. A key to successfully leading ourselves and others is learning Eternal principles and living in accordance with them. Eternal principles are like gasoline. An engine is made to run on gasoline, and it would not run properly on anything else. God designed the human machine to run on Eternal principles and it will not run properly on anything else. Eternal principles are directions for running the human machine. Eternal principles are there to prevent a breakdown, strain, or friction in the running of the human machine. When we violate Eternal principles, we cause trouble in the running of the human machine.[12] If we desire to obtain happiness and perfection, we have to live in accordance with Eternal principles for they are the recipe for obtaining happiness and eternal life.

We have the power to choose to obey or disobey Eternal principles, but we do not have the power to choose the consequences of our actions. Just as what we choose to eat determines what our physical body will be like, Eternal principles determine what our inner body—our character—will be like.

Each choice we make affects our character. Every time we make a choice we are either becoming a more godlike being or becoming a more hellish creature in nature. We are becoming a being that is in harmony with God, himself, and others or becoming a creature that is in a state of rebellion and hatred with God, himself, and others. As we obey Eternal principles, we move to a more godlike state. As we disobey, we become more hellish in nature. To be a godlike creature is joy, happiness, peace and power. To be a hellish creature is sadness, discord, hatred and weakness. Each moment we are progressing toward one of the these two states. Eternal principles are not only the directions for running the human machine; they also determine what kind of machines we become.

Learning Eternal principles in relation to leadership is extremely important today because everyone is reading and hearing things discussed about leadership. However, many of the ideologies being taught are false. Each year there seems to be a new way to lead others, a faster way, or an easier way. Many of the ideas being taught on leadership are ineffective or infused with the false philosophies of men.

We compare many of the ideas being taught on leadership to rocks. Many hear an idea on leadership and implement it into their life only to find out that it doesn't improve their life and may, in fact, worsen it. This is like a person planting a rock and then watering it and fertilizing it with no results. Have you ever planted and watered a rock? Of course not, because you know it will not grow. However, we bet many of you have planted what we call "leadership rocks." It can be hard to determine which leadership principles are rocks and which ones are seeds. As our leadership practices are founded on Eternal principles, we can know we are planting seeds which will grow and bring forth good fruit.

Knowledge: A Key Element of Effect Leaders

"Your mind is like a parchute. It only works when it is open."
—Lennon Ledbetter

"Keep your mind open to change all the time. Welcome it. Court it. It is only by examining and reexamining your opinions and ideas that you can progress."
—Dale Carnegie

Examples of Knowledge (things we know that affect the things we do): Understanding Gospel Doctrines Such as Divine Nature, All Men Are Created Equal, Diversity, Agency, Power to Choose, and Justification Through the Grace of Christ.

Knowledge is gaining an understanding of and belief in a principle. There are no "hows" to learn in gaining knowledge.

Many try to treat principles of knowledge as skills and are frustrated when they can't find a way to apply them in their daily life. They complain that the ideas are abstract and of no benefit—that they want to learn something they can do. They don't realize that gaining knowledge is one of the most powerful ways to improve their behavior and bring them success.

We often have people come to us and say, "This leadership stuff is great, but when do we get to try it out?" They want to know how to apply principles of knowledge such as agency. The answer is, you cannot. At least you can't apply it directly in the same way you apply skills such as delegation and goal setting. Principles of knowledge are not something you "do." They are something you "know." However, if you understand them, they will affect your actions. The way one applies principles of knowledge is by learning them. If you understand these principles, your decisions will become more sophisticated, and you will be more successful in life.

For example, if someone asked, "How can I apply the grace of Christ in my everyday life?" the person may get frustrated when you can't give him a specific answer. It's not that there isn't a good answer. It's a bad question. You can't directly do anything to apply Christ's grace in your life. You apply the grace of Christ by understanding it and believing it. When a person understands and believes in Christ's grace, he is filled with hope and relies on the merits of Christ, not his own. You can **know** the grace of Christ but you can't **do** the grace of Christ. However, understanding and believing in Christ's grace will change your behavior.

Another example would be asking the question, "How do I apply sunshine in my everyday life?" Can you identify things that you can directly do to apply sunshine in your daily life? Probably not. However, sunshine changes how you live your life and affects how you do things. For example, a person who knows about sunshine may wear sunglasses when he goes outside. So, is the person that wears sunglasses applying sunshine in his everyday life? No, he wears glasses because he understands sunshine. The way one applies sunshine is by understanding it. When one understands it he will do things differently, like wearing sunglasses outside. While wearing glasses is not a direct application of sunshine in his life, his behavior is driven by his knowledge about sunshine.

Sometimes people have a hard time seeing the significance of learning principles of knowledge because they don't see how they apply in daily life. However, if you look deeply at the principles of knowledge, you can see how a knowledge and belief in them changes behavior and are thus applied by simply knowing them. For example, Hitler believed "that the races were graded. There were, according to him, superior races and inferior races. The highest race, according to Adolf Hitler, was the Aryan race—the race destined to be masters. The lowest race were the Jews and blacks—those who, in Hitler's view, were the root of all of civilizations evils and ills."[13]

From Hitler's belief in graded races, can we predict his behavior? You bet we can and history is a documentation of the destruction his belief caused. Was Hitler's knowledge in accordance with Eternal principles? Obviously not and thus his success—if you can call anything he achieved success—was short lived and eventually resulted in his death. What would have been the key to transforming Hitler's behavior? It would have been to change his belief in graded races to a belief that all men are created equal. As taught Boyd K. Packer, "True doctrine, understood, changes attitude and behavior. The study of the doctrines of the gospel will improve behavior more quickly than a study of behavior will improve behavior…That is why we stress so forcefully the study of the doctrines of the gospel."[14]

The learning of principles of knowledge, such as diversity, agency and other doctrines of the gospel, are extremely important because they change the way we live. If we learn principles of knowledge founded in Eternal principles, we will live a more Christlike life. Our beliefs do determine our behavior. If we want to change our behavior, we first must change our thinking. If we change what we think and believe, we will change our destiny and the destiny of those around us. One of the great blessings in life is that we can change our whole outlook on life, change our whole destiny, change everything by changing our minds.

Skills: A Key Element of Effective Leaders

"Anyone can be successful because everything it takes to be successful can be learned."
– Lennon Ledbetter

Examples of Skills (things we do): Repentance, Fasting, Prayer, Living a Balanced Life, Communication, Managing Conflict,

Establishing Trust/Friendships, Giving Compliments, Leading by the Spirit, Goal Setting, Delegation, Time Management, Planning, Evaluating, Motivating, Organizing, Teaching/Training Others, and Problem Solving.

A skill is something we do. A mistake people make in teaching skills is that they do not teach all four aspects of the skill (what, why, when and how). To possess a skill is to know the what, why, when and how to do something. One example is the skill of changing a spark plug. A person must know what a spark plug is, why you would change a spark plug (for example, to make the car run better), when to change it, and how to change it.

For example, let's say you understand what delegation is and why it is important, but you don't know how to delegate effectively. You will want to utilize the skill of delegation, but you can't because you don't know how to. Or let's say you know how to effectively delegate, but you don't understand why you need to delegate or why delegation is important. You will know how to delegate, but you will have no desire to delegate and won't do it. If you tell someone what to do but don't teach them how, you will frustrate them. If you teach someone how to do something but not why, they will not do it.

Skills can increase our ability to lead and influence others, but without faith in Christ and a possession of godly attributes they are simply human techniques that go no deeper than the surface.

Attributes: A Key Element of Effective Leaders

"Your character is yours alone to build.
No one can injure your character but you."
– David B. Haight

Examples of Positive Attributes: Integrity, Vision, Faithful, Charitable, Virtuous, Knowledgable, Temperant, Patient, Humble, Diligence, Meekness, Mercy, Courageous, Trustworthiness, Loyalty, Confident, Kind, Friendly and Happy.

Attributes are the characteristics that define who we are. To be a Divine-Centered Leader it is not enough to do what you say and practice what you preach. You must **be** what you teach. For example, let's consider the principle of service. You can't just teach about service or tell others they need to do it. You can't merely go out and do service. You must be a service-oriented person. It must be a part of you. With this paradigm, you view service not as an action you do, but as a attribute you possess. Thus, Divine-Centered Leaders do not merely teach about and do service, they **are** service.

Attributes enable our leadership skills and attempts to influence others to become effective. Stephen Covey teaches the ineffectiveness of skills if not coupled with positive attributes: "To use human influence strategies and tactics of how to get people to do what I want, to work better, to be more motivated, to like me and each other—while my character is fundamentally flawed, marked by duplicity and insincerity—then, in the long run, I cannot be successful. My duplicity will breed distrust, and everything I do—even using so-called good human relations techniques—will be perceived as manipulative. It simply makes no difference how good rhetoric is or even how good the intentions are; if there is little or no trust, there is no foundation for permanent success. Only basic goodness gives life to technique."[15]

The elements of effective leadership are interrelated and have a synergistic relationship (synergy occurs when the whole is greater than the sum of its parts). Leaders must posses both attributes and skills to lead others. Skills without attributes results in failure, as will attributes without skills. The relationship between attributes and skills can be positively or negatively synergistic (negative synergy occurs when the whole is less than the sum of its parts). An example of synergy would be 2 x 8=16. The product of the two factors (16) is greater than the sum of the two factors (10). An example of negative synergy would be 8 x 0=0. The product of the two factors (0) is less than the sum of the two factors (8).

The following equation will help us to understand the relationship between attributes and skills— E(effectiveness) = A(attributes) x S(skills). This equation is used to illustrate the relationship between attributes and skills. It is not meant to be used for practical application. For illustration purposes, lets say we can rate our attributes and skills on a scale of 0 to 10. If our attributes rating is 0—no matter how high the skills rating—the effectiveness rating always results in zero. Also, if our skills rating is 0—no matter how high the attributes rating—the effectiveness rating always results in zero. If either or both factors is between 0 and 1, negative synergy will result. For example, your attribute rating is .5 and your skills rating is 8. The effectiveness rating (4) is less than the sum of the parts (8.5). If the rating of both factors is greater than one, synergy will result. For example, your attribute rating is 7 and your skills rating is 4. The effectiveness rating (28) is greater than the sum of the individual factors (11). Attributes and skills are required for success.

This book will present the key components of leadership we must possess to implement the Know, Go, Show leadership process. Each concept presented can be categorized into one of the four elements (Eternal principles, knowledge, attributes, or skills) of effective leaders.

Distinguishing between principles of knowledge and principles of skills is extremely important because it determines how the principle is to be taught and how it is to be learned. Throughout the book, the principles of knowledge are taught by presenting the whats and the whys of the principles with no discussion on how to apply the principles. The principles of skill will contain discussion on the whats, whys, whens and hows and will offer application ideas.

Let's begin our journey through the Know, Go, Show Process.

PART 3

Knowing the Way

STEP 3: ***Showing the Way***
Leading Others to Success

STEP 2: ***Going the Way***
Leading by Example, Being a Person of Intergrity

STEP 1: ***Knowing the Way***
Having Vison, Providing Direction and Purpose

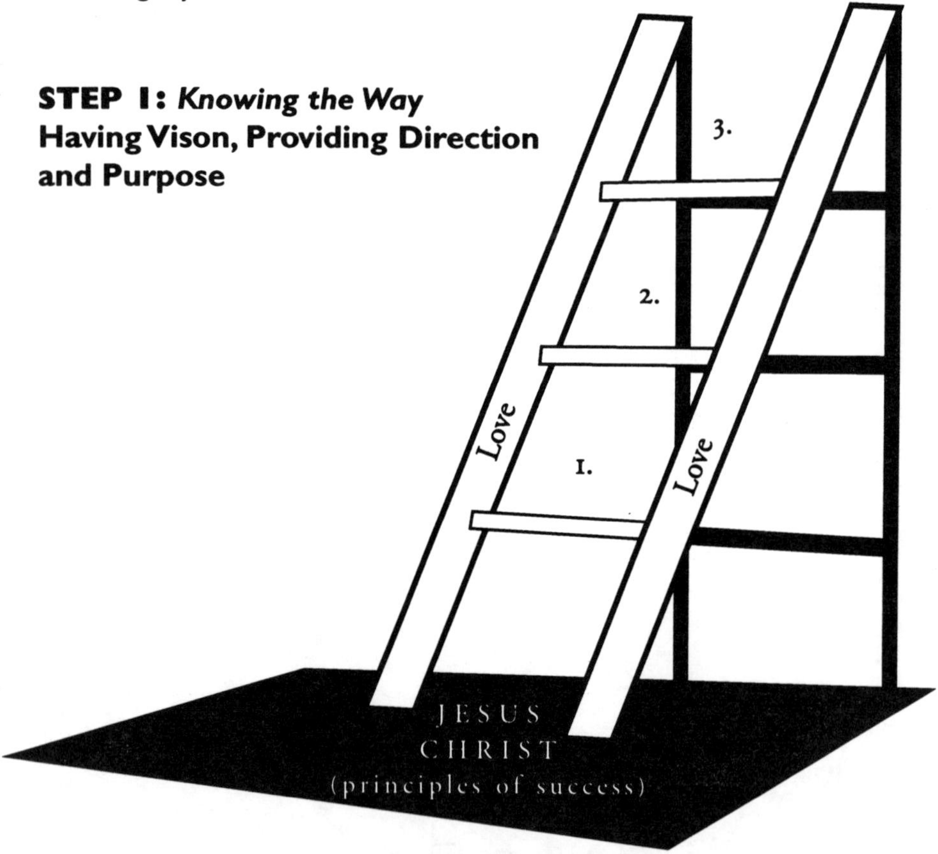

"It is upon the rock of our Redeemer who is Christ the Son of God that ye must build your foundation."

PART 3: KNOWING THE WAY

" We must have goals and dreams to make progress and achieve greatness."
—Lennon Ledbetter

Leaders are pioneers. Leaders take people places. However, we can't lead until we have somewhere to go. We've all heard the familiar saying, "a journey of a thousand miles begins with but a single step," but a journey of a thousand miles is pointless unless we know where we are going and why we want to get there. Divine-Centered Leaders know where they are going. They have vision, but it is not an ordinary vision, it is an inspired vision.

"There is no more powerful engine driving an organization toward excellence and long-range success than an attractive, worthwhile, and achievable vision of the future, widely shared."
—Burt Nanus

Where should Divine-Centered Leaders obtain their vision? Their vision is one of divine origin. It is Christ's vision. Divine-Centered Leaders seek to become one in purpose with Christ and seek to have their followers do the same. Divine-Centered Leaders have the "mind of Christ." "That is: They think what He thinks; they say what He says; they do what He does; and their souls are attuned to His—all because they live the way He lives and have acquired the same attributes and perfections that He possesses."[1]

Unity and the spirit of oneness should characterize Divine-Centered Leaders and their followers. The Lord has commanded, "Be one, and if ye are not one ye are not mine."[2] and "He that is not with me is against me."[3]

"If we are not united, we would not be the people of God. It is the true sign by which the people of God may be found. I do not care what we may claim or what our pretensions may be, we are not the people of God when we are not united."[4]

Christ further taught the principle of unity when he said, "Every kingdom divided against itself is brought to desolation; and every city or house divided against itself shall not stand."[5] He also reminded us that "No man can serve two masters: for either he will hate the one, and love the other; or else he will hold to the one, and despise the other."[6]

Divine-Centered Leaders should seek to become one with Christ as Christ is one with the Father. Christ has "in perfection, the mind of [His Father]. His words are their words, his thoughts are their thoughts. He represents Deity in his own right and He represents the composite glory, power, knowledge, and dominion of all that is Deity anywhere in the immensity of space."[7] Though separate in person, Christ and the Father are one in the implementation of their divine purpose to bring to pass the immortality and eternal life of men. This truth is reiterated in the scriptures. For example, in John 5:19 it says, "The Son can do nothing of himself, but what he seeth the Father do; for what things soever he doeth, these also doeth the Son likewise." (See also John 10:30, 38; 17:21) This unity between the Father and the Son serves as our example.

What was and is the source of Christ's greatness and unification? His Father. Christ was perfect because He lived in accordance with the will and mind of His Father, who has all knowledge and perfection. As His Father's will and mind became Christ's, they became perfectly unified. We too obtain greatness and unification by seeking Christ's mind and will, for He is perfect in knowledge and performance. As our will becomes Christ's desire, we have the "mind of Christ" and are unified with him. Developing the "mind of Christ" requires meekness—the ability to put the will of Christ above our own and seek God's will in all things. Meekness leads to greatness and unification. "Jesus, who was and is 'more intelligent than they all'[8], is also more meek than they all."[9] Perfect unity is found through complete obedience to Eternal principles.

Unity through Christ creates an environment of harmony, good will, peace, mutual understanding, love, and service—a state the human heart constantly yearns for. When unity is not present the environment is characterized by discord, contention, strife, confusion, and selfishness. Unity creates an atmosphere we all desire and love.

When we are unified, we are focusing our energies toward the same goal. When we are divided, that energy is instead being used to tear down the individual parts. "Certainly throughout all of human history this quality of unity or harmonious joint has proven to be one of the most important elements in any accomplishment. When men are not able to unite and work together, then those going in one direction tend to neutralize the efforts of those going in the opposite, direction, and the result is confusion and failure."[10] "When we act in a united effort, we create spiritual synergism, which is increased effectiveness or achievement as a result of combined action or cooperation, the result of which is greater than the sum of the individual parts."[11]

Vision Defined

"The only part of time that's of interest to me is the future. That's where I'm going to spend the rest of my life."
—Charles F. Kettering

We have discussed the importance of becoming one with Christ's purpose and connecting to his vision, but what exactly is vision? What are the characteristics of a leader with vision?

Vision is the ability to visualize the path ahead—to see things others don't and provide followers with direction. Vision is the ability to see the potential within each individual and in organizations and projects. A visionary leader believes there is no limit and that anything can be accomplished. Vision is the process of providing directions, comprehending an action's consequences and envisioning the desired end. Vision creates purpose, which creates action.

"To choose a direction, a leader must first have developed a mental image of a possible and desirable future state of the organization . . . The critical point is that a vision articulates a view of a realistic, credible, attractive future for the organization, a condition that is better in some important ways than what now exists. A vision is a target that beckons…A vision always refers to a future state, a condition that does not presently exist and never existed before. With a vision, the leader provides the all-important bridge from the present to the future of the organization…Great leaders often inspire their followers to high levels of achievement by showing them how their work contributes to worthwhile ends. It is an emotional appeal to some of the most fundamental of human needs—the need to be important, to make a difference, to feel useful, to be a part of a successful and worthwhile enterprise."[12]

Vision is the ability to see the potential of others and an ideal future state. Christ is all knowing. He sees the full potential within each person and completely understands the celestial state which is possible to obtain. Therefore, Christ is our perfect source of vision.

The Power of Vision

Divine-Centered Leaders "recognize that people need a vision of what they can do, of their true potential. Failing that, they will in all likelihood remain satisfied with the status quo and simply molder their lives away. 'Where there is no vision, the people perish.'[13]"[14]

People want direction and purpose but not all will cultivate within themselves a vision or purpose on their own. They need a leader to inspire them with a vision—to give them direction and purpose. As leaders rise up with a vision, they will have many followers for all people want to be involved in meaningful endeavors. People can accomplish great things when a leader shows them their potential and a desirable end.

Apathy, laziness, boredom and low self-esteem result from a lack of vision and purpose. As you provide individuals with vision and purpose, you will see new people emerge full of enthusiasm and drive, diligence and dedication to bring forth the vision. These attributes are within each individual. People simply need a reason to exhibit them. Vision attracts commitment, energizes, creates meaning, establishes a standard for excellence, and makes people transcend the status quo. Vision enables excellence and achievement.

Victor Frankl, an Austrian psychologist who survived the death camps of Nazi Germany, made a significant discovery. As he found within himself the capacity to rise above his humiliating circumstances, he became an observer as well as a participant in the experience. He watched others who shared in the ordeal. He was intrigued with the question of what made it possible for some people to survive when most died. He looked at several factors—health, vitality, family structure, intelligence, survival skills. Finally, he concluded that none of these factors was primarily responsible. The single most significant factor was a sense of future vision—the compelling conviction of survivors that they had a mission to perform, some important work left to do.[15]

Survivors of Prisoner of War camps in Vietnam and elsewhere have reported similar experiences: a compelling, future-oriented vision is the primary force keeping them alive.

The power of vision is incredible! Research indicates that children with "future-focused role images" perform far better scholastically and are significantly more competent in handling the challenges of life.[16] Teams and organizations with a strong sense of mission significantly outperform those without the strength of vision. According to Dutch sociologist Fred Polak, a primary factor influencing the success of civilizations is their "collective vision" of the future.[17]

Vision is the best manifestation of creative imagination and the primary motivation of human action. It's the ability to see beyond our present reality, to dream, to invent what does not yet exist, to become what we not yet are. It gives us capacity to live out of our imagination instead of our memory.[18]

Application Ideas for Gaining Vision

1. Create your own Statement of Excellence. Ladder of Success has developed a book to assist you in developing a Statement of Excellence. It can be purchased by calling 1-801-755-5323. A portion of the book on developing a Dream (Vision) Statement is included in the appendix on page 151. Create a Dream Statement using the materials in the appendix.

Goal Setting

> *"We must have goals to make progress, and it's encouraged by keeping records. Progress is easier when it is timed, checked, and measured. Goals should always be made to a point that*

will make us reach and strain. The key goals we could have are goals to be perfect in certain elements in our character, the things that we carry with us after this life."
—Spencer W. Kimball

Goal setting is the process of working toward our vision and dreams (fulfilling goals is not the process of setting goals) and bringing our lives into accordance with our values. Goal Setting has been found to be one of the most powerful ways to accomplish our dreams and desires. "At Yale University in 1953, the graduating class was polled to see how many had written goals that were definite, positive, specific, believable, desirable, and attainable. Only three percent had such goals. Twenty years later. This chronofile/longevity study was reopened, only to discover that the students with written goals had accomplished sum totally more than the other 97 percent of the class combined. The message is clear: Become a 'three percenter,' set goals. It's likely that by doing so you will become a super-achiever, big-time winner, and make a positive difference in life."[19] Make a commitment now to regularly set goals.

To be effective, the goals set must be challenging, attainable, written, measurable, and purposeful.

Challenging and Attainable: Goals should be challenging enough that people can obtain their full potential. Jesus set goals for us to help us reach our potential. "Be ye therefore perfect, even as your Father which is in heaven is perfect."[20] Christ knows our potential and He expects us to shoot for top performance and perfection. Leaders must set high goals but they must not be unattainable and discouraging. Goals should make people stretch and bring out their best. However, the leader needs to ensure that the goals are both challenging and attainable. As states Joe Paterno, "A coach has to set high goals ...he has to aim high, think big, and then make sure the players aspire to the highest goals they can achieve."

Written: All of us have goals, yet few of us have written goals. Studies show that when we write goals down we are significantly more likely to obtain them. Writing our goals helps us clearly define what we want to accomplish. An unwritten goal is merely a wish. Many people achieve little in life simply because they never decided to achieve something. Mark Victor Hasen in his book *Future Diary* says, "It grieves me to watch individuals squander their lives because they have neglected the process of writing down their personal goals." You can't review a goal that is not written. Written goals that are reviewed become reality.

Measurable: If you can't measure it, you can't achieve it. Goals must be measurable or there is no way to know when you have achieved it or how you are progressing. Measuring enables us to know where we currently are and enables us to see how we are progressing.

A simple example of this would be with dieting. I often hear people say, "I can't believe how much I weigh, I eat like a bird." A good place for this person to start is for a week to carry around a pad of paper and a pen and write down everything they eat or drink. This helps them become aware of how much food and what kind of food they are eating. Most of them find they are eating like a awfully big bird.

Purposeful: Goals must be working toward an aim or accomplishment. Don't confuse activity with accomplishment. Long-term goals should stem out of our vision, mission, and purpose. Short-term goals should work toward accomplishing long-term goals.

Often times we set and complete goals with no real accomplishment. The goal becomes an end in itself. For example, I (Cameron) was in a meeting with the church leaders of the Honolulu congregations. The meeting was to discuss how the members were progressing toward the goal of becoming more like Christ. The leaders felt this goal could be accomplished by increasing church attendance, home visits to the members, scripture reading (personal and family), prayer (personal and family), and by having a family night.

Each congregation kept statistics on all these numbers and, although there was improvement in all areas, there was no real growth in the church members. The members were doing more of the above items and doing them more often, but there was no real change. The leaders were perplexed by the results and began discussing why an increase in activities they thought would result in more Christlike living failed to do so. As the discussion developed, there was one point that hit the problem on the head.

The problem was that the goals of church attendance, home visits, scripture reading, prayer, and family night had become an end in themselves. The members viewed the goals as accomplished by simply doing them. They didn't use the goals to become more Christlike. Thus, the goals' completion provided the members with minimal benefit because they failed to connect the goals to the desired end and purpose. The things we do are not nearly as important as why we do them.

The Pharisees fell into a similar trap. They understood the law of Moses and how to obey it, but failed to understand that its purpose was to prepare them to live the gospel of Christ. They felt they were righteous simply by keeping the law of Moses. Therefore, they were unable to accept the gospel when presented to them because they had not accomplished the purpose behind living the law of Moses. Keeping the law of Moses was of no benefit to the Pharisees, and actually proved to be quite detrimental. Their belief that salvation came by the law alone resulted in them rejecting the Savior and His gospel.

We must guard against what we call the "checklist Christian" mentality. A checklist Christian feels if he can just complete the list of things God has told him to do (go to church, read scriptures, say prayers, pay tithing, help the poor), he will be saved. A checklist Christian believes he will be saved by what he does—not because of who he is. Who we are, not what we have done, determines our salvation. "For behold, God hath said a man being evil cannot do that which is good; for if he offereth a gift, or prayeth unto God, except he shall do it with real intent it profiteth him nothing. For behold, it is not counted unto him for righteousness. For behold, if a man being evil giveth a gift, he doeth it grudgingly; wherefore it is counted unto him the same as if he had retained the gift; wherefore he is counted evil before God."[21]

We can do all the good works in the world, but if it isn't helping us obtain the future end and purpose of becoming more Christlike and obtaining perfection, they are of no benefit. Paul taught this principle in 1 Corinthians 13:1, 3, "Though I speak with the tongues of men and of angels, and have not charity, I am become as sounding brass, or a tinkling cymbal… And though I bestow all my goods to feed the poor, and though I give my body to be burned, and have not charity, it profiteth me nothing."

"There is never achievement in any field of endeavor unless it is preceded by a strong sense of purpose. There must be reasons for action and guides for action in the form of real goals and objectives. That is why we are given a plan of salvation and progression. Because the gospel is a long-range even an eternal goal, it must be broken up into short-range, immediate objectives that can be achieved today and tomorrow and the next day. The gospel imperatives constitute an immediate challenge to action in our lives right now, today, as well as a plan for action eternally."[22]

Having purposeful goals is also important because the purpose provides us with motivation. The key to motivation is the "why." If you teach a man what to do and how to do it but fail to teach him why he should do it, he will have no motivation to accomplish the desired end.

Short-Term Goals

"When you see a man on top of a mountain, he didn't fall there."
—Lennon Ledbetter

Short-term goals can be accomplished within about a week and they help make your Statement of Excellence a reality. Short-term goals should work toward your long-term goals and stem directly from your Statement of Excellence. Short-term goals are of no value unless they are working toward an end and purpose. For more information about Statements of Excellence, call 1-801-755-5323.

Short-Term Goal Setting Workshop

Setting and accomplishing short-term goals can be best achieved by following an eight-step process.

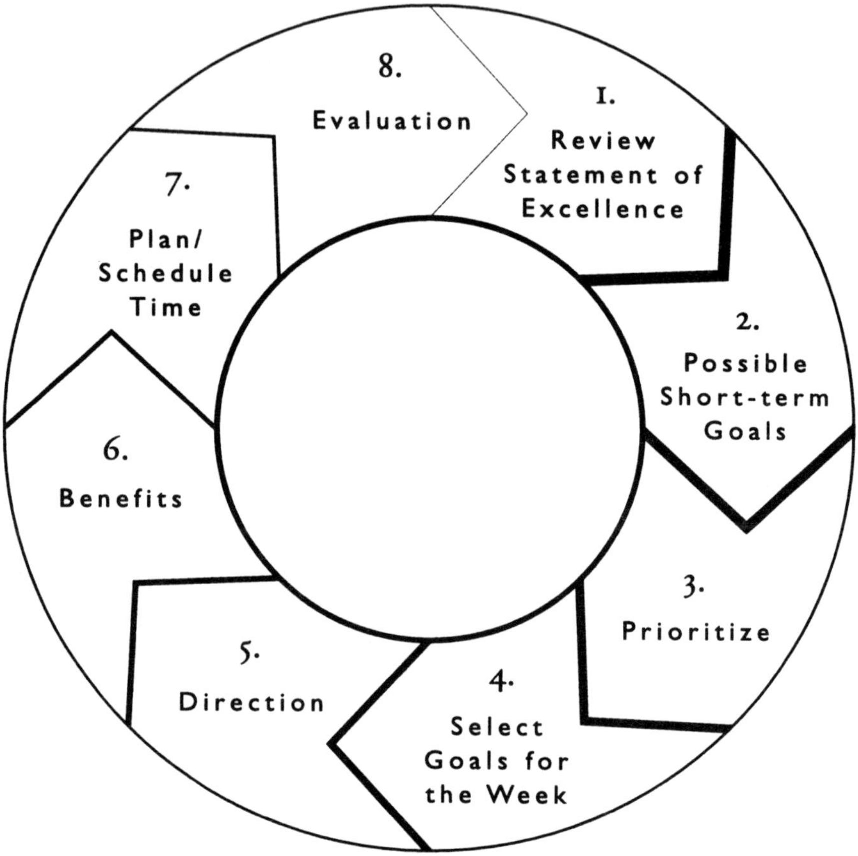

8 Step Goal Setting Process

Setting and accomplishing short-term goals can best be achieved by following an eight-step process.

1. *Review Statement of Excellence.* Short-term goals flow from your Statement of Excellence. Thus, the first step is to review your Statement of Excellence.

2. *Possible Short-Term Goals.* Identify possible short-term goals that will help you accomplish your Statement of Excellence. The short-term goals should be something you can complete within a week. You will set short-term goals in the four aspects of your life (intellectual, social, spiritual, and physical) and in each of your roles. This step can be done on the form entitled, "Possible Short-term Goals." Samples of this form are found on page 162.

Possible Short-term Goals / STEPS 2 & 3

ROLE: Personal Development			
Intellectual	Social	Physical	Spiritual
		exercise regularly	
		eat more fruits and veggies	
		eat less meat	
		take vitamins	

3. *Prioritize.* Prioritize your possible short-term goals to identify which goals will be the most beneficial. You can do this by numbering them from 1 to 10 with 1 being the most important.

Possible Short-term Goals / STEPS 2 & 3

ROLE: Personal Development			
Intellectual	Social	Physical	Spiritual
		1 exercise regularly	
		3 eat more fruits and veggies	
		4 eat less meat	
		2 take vitamins	

4. *Select Goals for the Week.* Steps 4 through 8 are to be completed on the form entitled "Short-Term Goal Setting Process." Samples of the form are found on page 164 . From your list of possible short-term goals, select goals to focus on for the week.

5. *Direction.* For each goal you set for the week, identify the long-term goal you are working towards.

6. *Benefits.* For each goal you set for the week, identify its benefits.

7. *Plan.* Develop a plan to accomplish the short-term goals during the week. What do I need to do? How much time do I need to spend? When I am going to do it?

8. *Evaluation.* Evaluation enables you to chart your progress and identify reasons why you are or are not accomplishing your goals. Evaluation enables you to learn from living and identify areas where you can still improve. Evaluation also enables you to adjust your goals to current circumstances.

Set up a time when you will evaluate your performance for the week. Compare your actual results against your goals. What kept me from accomplishing my goals? What enabled me to accomplish my goals? Are my goals realistic? Are my goals challenging? Am I spending enough time doing the things that are truly important to me?

Evaluation sets you up to begin the process again. From your evaluation, you determine which goals will stay the same in the next week, which goals to adjust, and then begin the process again at step number 1.

An example of the process:

1. *Review Statement of Excellence.* Within your Statement of Excellence, you have a long-term goal to be physically fit.

2. *Possible Short-Term Goals.* You determine you could exercise regularly, eat more fruits and vegetables, eat less meat, and take

Short-Term Goal Setting Process / STEPS 4 – 8

STEP 1:Review Statement of Excellence

STEP 2:Set possible short-term goals (Refer to "Possible Short-term Goal Form")

STEP 3:Prioritize possible short-term goals (Refer to Possible "Short-term Goal Form")

Date: Month/Date Role: Personal Development: Physical Evaluation (day/time): Sun 10p.m.

STEP 4: Weekly Goal

Exercise

STEP 5: Direction

I am exercising so I can develop and maintain a healthy body and be physically fit.

STEP 6: Benefits

controls weight, improves muscle tone, increases flexibility, improves quality of sleep, increases confidence and self-esteem, makes me happier and more alert intellectually, socially, and spiritually

STEP 7: Plan / Schedule Time

Schedule time Monday through Friday from 8-9 a.m. to exercise. Run two miles each morning.

STEP 8a: Actual Results

I ran Monday, Wednesday, and Thursday and slept in the other days.

STEP 8b: Evaluation

It was hard to get up in the morning. I may be more successful scheduling time to run at night. I don't like running. Maybe instead of running, I could play basketball. I am going to keep the goal to exercise every week, but I am going to adjust the plan to complete the goal by scheduling time to run at night and begin playing basketball some of the nights.

vitamins to accomplish this long-term goal. Use form "Possible Short-Term Goals."

3. *Prioritize.* You prioritize your short term goals from most important to least important: exercise, take vitamins, eat fruits and vegetables, eat less meat. Use form "Possible Short-term Goals."

4. *Select Goals for the Week.* You decide that this week you are going to start exercising regularly. Use form entitled, "Short-term Goal Setting Process" for steps 4 through 8. See example form on page 46.

5. *Direction.* I am exercising regularly so I can develop and maintain a healthy body and be physically fit.

6. *Benefits.* Regular exercise helps control weight, improve muscle tone, increase flexibility, improve quality of sleep, increase confidence and self-esteem, makes me happier and more alert intellectually, socially, and spiritually.

7. *Plan.* Schedule time Monday through Friday from 8-9 a.m. to exercise. Run two miles each morning.

8. *Evaluation.* On Sunday evening at 10 p.m., I will evaluate my actual performance compared to my goal. I set a goal to run two miles Monday through Friday. I actually ran Monday, Wednesday and Thursday and slept in the other days. It was extremely hard to get up in the morning. I may want to consider scheduling time to run at night. I didn't enjoy running, so maybe I could do something I like better, such as basketball. I am going to keep the goal to exercise regularly every week, but I am going to adjust the plan of how I will complete the goal by scheduling time to run at night and begin playing basketball on some of the nights.

Following the eight step process of goal setting allows us to implement our Statement of Excellence. Following the process ensures that we are doing the things that are truly important to us and will result in the kind of life we want to enjoy.

Ideas to Remember When Following the Goal-Setting Process

Be Flexible

To make goals both challenging and attainable takes continual adjustment. These adjustments are done during the evaluation step of the process. Leaders need the vision to see necessary adjustments and facilitate them.

Continually Follow the Process

The eight step goal-setting process needs to be followed each week. It is a process of continually working toward your vision.

"Every time the Japanese attain a goal for quality, cost, or innovation, they ask themselves, How can we do it better? How can we improve? They are never satisfied with the status quo or with past attainments. Reaching a goal is merely a signal to set a higher one, goal-setting is done in small increments so that people never become discouraged: at the same time, they are never permanently satisfied. The Japanese vision is of a never-ending quest for improvement both in work process and in outcomes."[23]

You Must Commit to Your Goals

You may have set wonderful goals, but if there is no commitment, zero to minimal action will occur. If you are setting personal goals, you should make a conscious commitment to achieve them. If you are setting the goals within a group or organization, it is important to involve all that will be working toward the goal. As you involve people in the goal setting process, you will greatly increase their level of commitment. People are more interested and committed to their own ideas and goals.

"An effective [goal] has two dimensions; quality and commitment. By weighing these two dimensions and multiplying them, we can determine the effectiveness factor. For example, let's suppose that we make a quality [goal]—a perfect 10 on a 10-point scale; however, for some reason the commitment to that decision is low—a 2 on a 10-point scale. As a result we have a relatively ineffective [goal] (by multiplying 10 and 2, we get an effectiveness factor of 20). Now let's assume that by involving others, we compromise the quality of the [goal] (it drops from 10 down to 7), but we increase the commitment to it (let's say from 2 to 8). In this case, we have an effectiveness factor of 56 (7 times 8). That means the [goal] may not be as good, but it is almost three times as effective! Nonetheless, many young or new managers hesitate to involve people in [goal setting] for fear of opening up other options, contaminating their own thinking, or compromising their position. Eventually, through experience, most managers learn that the effectiveness of their [goals] depends on quality and commitment, and that commitment comes through involvement. They are then willing to assume the risks and to develop the skills of involving people appropriately."[24]

For example, let's say you set a long-term goal to be physically fit, and you feel the best way to be physically fit is to run everyday. However, you hate running and dread doing it. So, using the equation Quality X Commitment = Effectiveness, you may have a quality factor of 10 but a commitment factor of 2 resulting in an effectiveness rating of 20. You also think you could play basketball everyday to be physically fit. You feel this will not be as effective of a workout, but you love to play basketball and like to play whenever you can. Using the formula Quality X Commitment = Effectiveness, you may have a quality rating of 7 and a commitment rating of 9 resulting in effectiveness rating of 63. The goal to play basketball daily has an effectiveness rating more than three time that of running daily because of increased commitment.

Remove Restraining Forces

Often times there are forces that keep us from obtaining our goals. We should identify what these forces are and seek to remove them. For example, let's say we are driving a car with the emergency brake on. The emergency brake is a restraining force. By identifying the problem and taking the emergency break off, we will increase our driving speed and performance.

For example, television is a force that keeps a lot of people from achieving their goals and dreams. Television is the greatest tool Satan has to keep people mediocre. If television is a force keeping you from your goals and dreams, you may want to remove it from your home. Another option would be to define what your dreams and goals are and then tape them to the front of your TV screen. Then if you are tempted to waste an evening watching TV, you must first peel away your goals and dreams before you begin watching.

Increase Your Ability to Accomplish Goals

As we set goals, there are two types we should set. One helps to accomplish our goal, and the other increases our ability to accomplish it. An example would be:

Goal	**Goal That Increases Our Ability to Accomplish**
Exercise Regularly	Go to the library and learn more about exercising effectively.

Exercising regularly directly helps you accomplish the long-term goal of being physically fit. As you learn more about exercise, you will increase your ability to exercise in a way that will help you obtain that long-term goal.

Application Ideas for the Goal Setting Process

1. Schedule a time each week to complete the goal setting process.

PART 4

Going the Way

STEP 3: ***Showing the Way***
Leading Others to Success

STEP 2: ***Going the Way***
Leading by Example, Being a Person of Intergrity

STEP 1: ***Knowing the Way***
Having Vison, Providing Direction and Purpose

"It is upon the rock of our Redeemer who is Christ the Son of God that ye must build your foundation."

PART 4: GOING THE WAY

"A leader constantly seeks ways to do better whatever needs to be done. If a person with this quality will continue positive application of this negative factor, that person will have a leadership role. The quality: dissatisfaction. To make the unsatisfactory satisfactory or better is the mark of leadership. Never be satisfied with less than top performance, and progress will be the reward."
—Vince Lombardi

People who have vision but no action are dreamers not leaders. The second step of leadership is one of personal development (learning, doing, becoming). The process of personal development then places you in a position to help others. Divine-Centered Leaders go before their followers. "They recognize that they have the power to direct their lives—that their situations are a result of their choices, not circumstances. Thus, they take the initiative to make situations better and correct problems. They continually challenge their shortcomings by sincerely repenting. They never become satisfied with less than top performance. They seek excellence and the elimination of mediocrity. As did Christ in cleansing the temple, they appropriately challenge the unrighteousness of others. They lead by example. They do more than simply practice what they preach—they are what they teach. They lead by the spirit—doing what Christ would do. They are full of integrity—they seek to live a life as Christ lived in accordance with principles and divine direction. They model how to live a balanced life, developing and managing the spiritual, social, intellectual, and physical elements of their lives."[1]

The elements of effective leadership needed to Go The Way that we will discuss are: agency, the power to choose, the need for initiative, our circle of responsibility, excellence, how to effectively manage conflict, leading by example, leading by the spirit, integrity, and living a balanced life.

Agency

"Know this, that every soul is free, to choose his life and what he'll be; for this eternal truth is given, that God will force no man to heaven. He'll call, persuade, direct aright, and bless with wisdom, love and light; in nameless ways be good and kind but never force the human mind."—William C. Gregg.

Agency is a gospel principle that makes it possible for us to Go the Way. It gives us the power to progress and improve our lives and the lives of those around us. It is an eternal principle that has always existed and always will. Agency is the right to choose between good and evil. "Four great principles must be in force if there is to be agency: 1. Laws must exist, laws ordained by an Omnipotent power, laws which can be obeyed or disobeyed; 2. Opposites must exist—good and evil, virtue and vice, right and wrong—that is, there must be an opposition, one force pulling one way and another pulling the other; 3. A knowledge of good and evil must be had by those who are to enjoy the agency, that is, they must know the difference between the opposites; and 4. An unfettered power of choice must prevail."[2]

When we choose to live according to God's plan for us, our agency is strengthened. Right choices increase our power to make more right choices. Wrong choices limit our choices. "The following example suggests how this works. Imagine seeing a sign on the seashore that reads: 'Danger—whirlpool. No swimming allowed here.' We might think that is a restriction. But is it? We still have many choices. We are free to swim somewhere else. We are free to watch the sunset. We are free to go home. We are also free to ignore the sign and swim in the dangerous place. But once the whirlpool has us in its grasp and we are pulled under, we have very few choices. We can try to escape, or we can call for help, but we may drown."[3] "The great gift of agency is like fire: if properly controlled it becomes an agency of life; if improperly used it becomes the agency of death."[4]

We have the power to choose our actions, but we do not have the power to choose their consequences. The consequences, whether good or bad, follow as a natural result of any choice we make. For example, we can choose to touch a hot stove, but we cannot choose whether or not to get burned.

Power to Choose

"Life is a series of decisions we make. We live the life that we live because of the choices we have made."
—Lennon Ledbetter

Agency provides us with the ability to achieve greatness, but it also gives us the power to destroy ourselves. "Every time we make a choice we are turning the central part of us, the part of us that chooses, into something a little different from what it was before. And taking our life as a whole, with all our innumerable choices, all our life long we are slowly turning this central thing either into a heavenly creature or into a hellish creature; either into a creature that is in harmony with God, and with other creatures and with itself, or else into one that is in a state of war and hatred with God, and with its fellow-creatures, and with itself. To be the one kind of creature is heaven: that is, it is joy and peace and knowledge and power. To be the other means madness, horror, idiocy, rage, impotence, and eternal loneliness. Each of us at each moment is progressing to the one state or the other."[5]

Agency not only enables the power to choose between good and evil but also gives us the power to choose how we respond to various situations and stimuli. We are all influenced by external stimuli. But it is not what happens to us, but our response to it that determines how the stimuli affects us. As Eleanor Roosevelt observed, "No man can hurt you without your consent." In the words of Gandhi, "They cannot take away our self respect if we do not give it to them." Of course, things can hurt us physically or economically and can cause sorrow. But our character, our basic identity, our happiness, does not have to be hurt at all.[6]

We have the ability to choose how we respond to negative stimulus such as bad weather, people yelling or saying bad things about us, not accomplishing purposes, etc. None of these stimuli can make us sad, angry, or frustrated unless we choose to respond that way. Choose now to be happy no matter what the circumstances, and you will always be happy. Happiness doesn't depend on outward conditions but on the conditions inside.

Jesus is our best example. On the cross, though experiencing superhuman pain and suffering, he never became angry at his executors; instead he plead for forgiveness in their behalf. "Then said Jesus, Father, forgive them; for they know not what they do."[7] When His Jewish captors spit on, smote, and scourged Jesus during and after His trail, he didn't seek revenge or express hatred. Jesus was always in control of his emotions and no external force could make him express hatred. Jesus manifested charity in all circumstances and situations. It was his ability to choose righteous responses, in part, that made the Savior perfect. Though he was "in all things tempted like we are,"[8] he chose not to respond in ways that hurt others.[9]

We can choose to be like a thermometer or to be like a thermostat. A thermometer just sits there and measures what happens around it. It simply responds to its environment. If it is hot outside, it says it's hot. If it's cold outside, it says it's cold. A thermostat, on the other hand, measures what the temperature is and then responds by changing the temperature to the conditions it desires. If it wants it to be cooler, it turns on the air conditioner and cools it down. If it wants the temperature to be warmer, it turns on the heater. Most people are like a thermometer. If their environment is negative, they are negative. If bad things happen, they are sad. If good things happen, they are happy. They simply are a product of their environment. Divine-Centered Leaders are more like the thermostat. They seek to control they environment. Even if their environment is negative, they choose to be positive.

As we understand our power to choose, we see that we are in control. We have the ability to determine the kind of life we want to live and the type of person we wish to be, but obtaining all this requires effort and initiative. Becoming Christlike and helping others do the same requires us to take that initiative.

Taking the Initiative

"You can pay the price for success or you will pay the price of failure."—Lennon Ledbetter

Divine-Center Leaders take the initiative to create action, make improvements, and correct problems. "When we think of leaders, we recall times of turbulence, conflict, innovation, and change. We think of people who triumphed against overwhelming odds, who took initiative when there was inertia, who confronted the established order, who rose to the challenge of adversity, who mobilized people and institutions in the face of strong resistance. We think of people who generated momentum in society and then guided that energy toward a more fulfilling future."[10]

Christ took the initiative to create change and improvement. John 2:13-16 and Matthew 21:12-13 gives the account of Jesus cleansing the temple and casting out the money changers. "And the Jews' Passover was at hand, and Jesus went up to Jerusalem, And found in the temple those that sold oxen and sheep and doves, and the changers of money sitting: And when he had made a scourge of small cords, he drove them all out of the temple, and the sheep, and the oxen; and poured out the changers' money, and overthrew the tables; And said unto them that sold doves, Take these things hence; make not my Father's house an house of merchandise." "And said unto them, It is written, My house shall be called the house of prayer; but ye have made it a den of thieves." When Christ identified the problem of buying and selling at the Temple, he immediately took action to correct the problem even though it required great effort and risk.

If there are things in your personal life you don't like or know you should change or improve, you should take the initiative to make those changes. If you identify that you respond to a particular stimuli in a negative manner, you can take the initiative to change that behavior. For example, when you drive in traffic you get frustrated and angry. Make a mental effort to be happy and courteous when you drive, and do not let any outside stimuli—such as being cut off or people driving slowly—get you mad and frustrated. Divine-Centered Leaders never say, "That is just the way I am," or "There is nothing I can do about it." Divine-Centered Leaders take the initiative and make the effort required to improve and achieve the best that is within themselves, others, and organizations.

We have identified that change can occur and that Divine-Centered Leaders have a responsibility to seek improvement, but to what extent are we responsible for changing the world? What lies within our circle of responsibility?

Circle of Responsibility

"Almost everyone can do or be something for someone else in need."
—Joy F. Evans

What is the size of our circle of direct responsibility, our stewardship? What is the size of the circle of responsibility that includes problems and issues beyond our present control? Where do these circles overlap? How are our circles changing?

Often, our vision tends to be too narrow. We cannot allow the world's issues to become completely irrelevant to our lives. Our circle of responsibility increases as we recognize a spiritual reality absent in the vision most people have of the world. We must see our "circle of responsibility" as broadly as possible. John Donne wrote, "No man is an island, entire of itself; every man is a piece of the continent, a part of the main. If a clod be washed away by the sea, Europe is the less . . ."

We have concerns in the various roles and responsibilities of our lives—personal, work, family, community, national problems (crime, poverty, flood victims, lack of health care, sex discrimination, unwed/teenage mothers, violence, drugs, etc.), worldwide problems (world hunger, the status of women in Islamic countries, AIDS, ozone layer, etc.). How do each of these different problems affect us? Do we care, and if so, how much? What are we willing to sacrifice to correct them? What is our responsibility in correcting these problems?

Often we will hear people complain of the awful state of the country, yet when asked what they are doing about it they reply,

Circle of Responsibility Table

Circles of Responsibility	What is your Concern?	How much are you doing?	What more can you do?
SELF		1 2 3 4 5 6 7 8	
		1 2 3 4 5 6 7 8	
		1 2 3 4 5 6 7 8	
WORK		1 2 3 4 5 6 7 8	
		1 2 3 4 5 6 7 8	
		1 2 3 4 5 6 7 8	
FAMILY		1 2 3 4 5 6 7 8	
		1 2 3 4 5 6 7 8	
		1 2 3 4 5 6 7 8	
COMMUNITY		1 2 3 4 5 6 7 8	
		1 2 3 4 5 6 7 8	
		1 2 3 4 5 6 7 8	
NATIONAL ISSUES		1 2 3 4 5 6 7 8	
		1 2 3 4 5 6 7 8	
		1 2 3 4 5 6 7 8	
WORLD ISSUES		1 2 3 4 5 6 7 8	
		1 2 3 4 5 6 7 8	
		1 2 3 4 5 6 7 8	
OTHER		1 2 3 4 5 6 7 8	
		1 2 3 4 5 6 7 8	
		1 2 3 4 5 6 7 8	
		1 2 3 4 5 6 7 8	
		1 2 3 4 5 6 7 8	
		1 2 3 4 5 6 7 8	

"nothin'." Do we often fall in the same category? For example, are we registered to vote, do we write letters to our congressmen, do we actively support those whom we believe would make a good elected official? What is our responsibility in finding ways we can serve?

We need look no further than our immediate surroundings for people to serve. All around us, we have homeless, undernourished, those in need of medical aid and much more. How can we actively serve those around us? What can we do to truly make a difference right now in some of the pressing social situations surrounding us?

Application Ideas for Circle of Responsibility

Hopefully, these question have sparked some thought and desire to improve areas in your circle of responsibility. The table on page 60 will help you to identify problems that concern you and what you can do to make a difference. Enlarging your circle of responsibility will help you Go the Way.

Excellence: An Attribute of Divine-Centered Leaders

"Life is a competition not with others, but with ourselves. We should seek each day to live stronger, better, truer lives; each day to master some weakness of yesterday; each day to repair a mistake; each day to surpass ourselves."
—David B. Haight

"Winners don't just happen, they evolve."
—Spencer Taylor

One of the most important attributes we can develop is the attitude of improvement. Leaders envision the ideal and are never satisfied until they obtain this ideal. Leaders are constantly seeking to make improvements. "Leadership should seek to create a climate in which the leader and members of the group bring forth the best they have to offer. Sometimes, of course, the best which individuals have to offer is not of a high quality, but we must assure them as to the acceptability of their offering. Our task is avoiding unnecessary mediocrity, too, and our tolerance of poor performance by ourselves and others is, at times, not tolerance at all, but lazy leadership. By setting [our organizations] standards clearly and helping ourselves and others to grow within these standards in mind-stretching and ability-stretching ways we will experience infinite variety in outcome, but for the individual, this can result in closing the gap between what he is and what he might be."[11]

Perfection is the goal of Divine-Centered Leaders. Perfection will never be attained in this life, so our actual performance will always be below our ideal. However, "great men don't allow themselves to become discouraged. Their impatience with their own failings is tempered by an understanding that they are growing. While they are not unmindful of their weaknesses, they do not allow their lack of accomplishments to cast a shadow over their will to perform."[12] Our goal is perfection, but Christ is more worried about our desire to obtain perfection and our improvement than he is about our current performance.

The Lord expects us to continually seek improvement. The Lord rebukes those with apathy and contentment, those who are satisfied with their condition in life, who are content with the way things are, who don't seek change and improvement. "Therefore, wo be unto him that is at ease in Zion! Wo be unto him that crieth: All is well! Yea, wo be unto him that hearkeneth unto the precepts of men, and denieth the power of God, and the gift of the Holy Ghost! Yea, wo be unto him that saith: We have received, and we need no more! And in fine, wo unto all those who tremble, and are angry because of the truth of God! For behold, he that is built upon the rock receiveth it with gladness; and he that is built upon a sandy foundation trembleth lest he shall fall. Wo be unto him that shall say: We have received the word of God, and we need no more of the word of God, for we have enough!"[13]

We are always in need of improvement. If we say I "have need of nothing" and don't recognize that we are "wretched, and miserable, and poor, and blind and naked:", the Lord will see us a being lukewarm (apathetic). The Lord desires a non-apathetic people. For if we become neither hot nor cold, the Lord will spew us out of his mouth.[14]

The Lord illustrates how he feels about those who improve their condition in life and those who do not in the parable of the talents. In the parable, a lord gave to one of his servants five talents, to another two talents, and to another one. The servants who received two and five talents both return to the Lord more talents than he had given them to which the lord replied, "Well done, [thou] good and faithful servant: thou hast been faithful over a few things, I will make thee ruler over many things: enter thou into the joy of thy lord."[15] The servant who received one talent returned to the lord only the one talent he had received, for which he was rebuked by the lord. "His lord answered and said unto him, [Thou] wicked and slothful servant, thou knewest that I reap where I sowed not, and gather where I have not strawed: Thou oughtest therefore to have put my money to the exchangers, and [then] at my coming I should have received mine own with usury...And cast ye the unprofitable servant into outer darkness: there shall be weeping and gnashing of teeth."[16]

If we improve our condition while in this life, we can expect to receive the warm greeting of the Savior, "Well done, thou good and faithful servant." If we do not, we can expect to hear the rebuke as the Lord calls us wicked and slothful servants.

The Savior further teaches the need to strive for excellence in the miracle and parable of the fig tree in Mark 11:12-14. Jesus is walking along with His disciples and they come to a fig tree which has no figs on it. When Jesus saw that there were no figs upon the fig tree, He curses the fig tree and the next day it is withered up and dead. I often wondered what is the significance of this miracle. This miracle is different from all the other recorded miracles of Jesus which were performed for relief, blessing and beneficent purposes. This one appears to be an act of judgement and destructive execution. I had read this passage several times trying to understand what this miracle and parable meant but overlooked one passage key to its understanding. Verse thirteen says, "for the time of figs was not yet." The fig tree didn't have figs on it because figs were not in season. I thought, "Why was Jesus so hard on the tree? None of the trees had figs on them. Why did He destroy this one?" I began to pray for understanding of these scriptures and continually wondered what it meant.

One day I was driving in my car listening to a tape called "A Higher Standard of Excellence" by an inspired man, Mark Gorman, and he began to discuss the parable of cursing the fig tree. As he began to explain the revelation he received concerning the meaning of this miracles and parable, the spirit filled my soul and my mind was enlightened. Mark states on the tape that at two a clock in the morning God told him the meaning of these passages. When the inspiration came, he sat strait up in bed and God spoke to him saying, "If all you are doing is what comes naturally to you, I am not impressed. If you are only producing when everyone else is producing, so what. If you are just keeping up with the crowd, big deal."

If we are to impress the Lord, we must strive for excellence. We must do more than just what comes naturally to us. We must rise above average. We must rise above mediocrity. We must rise above just getting by. We must excel. We must excel. We must not just produce fruit when it is in season—we must produce fruit everyday.

Sterling W. Sill gives us additional insights on Excellence. The following is from his book *Leadership,* Vol. 3, p. 57-63.

A number of years ago, the Chesapeake and Potomac Telephone Companies ran a series of ads under the general title "The Quest for Excellence." Because of what appears to be a lowering of standards in so many areas of present-day activity, these four ordinary words could also serve as the heading under which some of the values in our own lives may be analyzed and upgraded. If it is profitable to develop excellence in a telephone company, it is many times more profitable to develop it in the government, the Church and our personal lives.

Whatever the field of our endeavor, success always shines its spotlight on quality. An increase in the excellence of a person's life goes far beyond increases that may be brought about in his finances. Excellence not only improves and beautifies, it motivates individuals who are concerned with it and helps to bring about greater accomplishment.

The idea of excellence comes very near to being the purpose of life itself, and for that reason it runs through everything we do. Every business and every professional group and every worthwhile social unit is conducting a constant search for quality. Quality is what we are attracted to and what we are inspired by. It is what we want in an automobile, in a home, and in a family. It is what we look for in everything we do, in everything we are, and in everything we ever hope to become.

Probably no other theme has gripped the American imagination so intensely as the discovery of outstanding character qualities or genuine talent in unexpected places. We are thrilled when someone from the slums becomes a scientific genius. We are delighted to hear of frail youngsters developing great athletic skills or to see poor boys become captains of industry. One history of excellence tells of a group of humble, unlearned fishermen and tax collectors who became saints and apostles.

Important points about the quest for excellence are that everyone is involved and that each person may direct his compass toward the goal of the greatest interest. It is a revered tradition in America that "anybody can become somebody." Our literature is filled with heroes and heroines. Everyone of us has been given a divine gift in the form of a strong inclination to lift himself upward by following an ideal. It is a profitable undertaking to hold in our minds the images of great thinkers, great doers, and great prophets. As we pay homage to the honesty of Abraham Lincoln and to the devotion of Paul the apostle, we become the beneficiaries of both. No one can hold a good idea in his mind or cherish a noble ambition in his heart without gaining from it. No one can do a good deed or discover a more effective way to render a service without himself being lifted up and made better.

A hundred years ago, Horatio Alger stimulated the ambitions of many young Americans with his "rags to riches" success stories. But excellence does not merely mean going from rags to riches. Its course also runs from "log cabin to president" from "plowboy to prophet," from "darkness to light," from "depression to happiness," and from "bad to good." The quest for excellence encourages self-discovery, awakens ambition, arouses industry, inspires emulation, and improves every accomplishment. Everyone has within himself a vein of greatness, and, more often than not, it is a touch of excellence that leads to its discovery. It is not unusual for one who has won outstanding success to say, "I never dreamed that it could happen to me," or, "I didn't think I had it in me." But excellence has the power to create success or bring it to the surface, it also teaches us how to engineer the shaft so that we may draw out the gold.

While speaking on the campus of Stanford University in 1906, William James said, "The world is only beginning to see that more than about anything else the wealth of nations consists in the number of superior men it harbors." When God created man in his own image and endowed him with miraculous faculties, it was his desire to fill the earth with superior men. God does not want us to become trapped in treacherous down drafts that thrust so many people into a state of mediocrity and depression. The purpose for the organization of the Church upon the earth was to build excellence in the Lord's children for both here and hereafter.

Of course, the first step in producing excellence is to believe in it. Frequently people are ashamed to be outstanding. It seems to much more comfortable to be mediocre. There is constant pressure pushing people toward being average. And when one has average goals and average ambitions, excellence becomes very difficult to achieve. Satan makes peoples content in just getting by. This is the way in which myriads of people are prevented from finding life's proper meaning. Too often we join some "cult of easiness" or attempt to find happiness in apathy, aimlessness, and the pursuit of lesser things and lower goals. As a result, we contract that widespread disease which surely is some variety of the inferiority complex.

John W. Gardner wrote a great book entitled *Excellence*. It's purpose is to help us orient our lives toward living at our best. He points out that while we have always paid the most pious lip service to the idea of excellence, we have really trifled with it in actual practice. There can be no real success or happiness without excellence, however, and there can be no excellence without intelligent effort.

Because every worthwhile thing in life is at stake, we should prepare our minds, our muscles, our hearts, our attitudes, and our spirits themselves for the promotion of excellence. Exceptions should not be tolerated. If anything is worth doing it is worth doing well, and we cannot personally afford to practice any degree of mediocrity. [Heaven] is the ultimate result of excellence. We must not send back to God a life that has only been half used. The greatest waste in the world is not the devastation of war; it is not the cost of crime; it is not the erosion of our soils; nor is it the depletion of our raw material, nor the loss of our gold supply. The greatest waste in the world is that human beings, you and I, live so far below the level of our possibilities. Compared with what we might be, we are just partly alive.

Excellence is a curiously powerful word. It can overcome all of life's down drafts. As we absorb the spirit of excellence, we can perform almost any miracle. When we develop a strong, deep feeling about it the most vigorous work becomes easy, and greater ambitions and more worthwhile interests follow in due course.

Excellence means different things to different people. To some it means to become a great scholar or a fine athlete, or to develop a noble character. To some, excellence may symbolize the golden age of Greece, or it may make us more aware of the problems of our own day and help us to weave into our own aspirations those specific activities necessary to create the better world we ourselves expect to help build.

The power drawing us upward is the pattern of excellence in him who was ordained to be our example. The mission of the Son of God was to redeem us from death and to help us live so that God's will could be done on earth as it is done in heaven. When this kind of quest is accompanied by the proper amount of searching, aspiring, and longing, it produces an affinity for good that can bring us back to God. For this purpose the Creator has placed within us an upward reach, an improvement instinct, a divine urge for superiority that should have our constant encouragement.

When enough strength is given to this ambition to do our best, it gives dignity and character to our work, pleasure to our hearts, and happiness to our families. Whether one works as a janitor, a judge, a surgeon, a technician, or whatever work he may do, his life, to be complete, must have excellence. When anyone does a slovenly, dishonest, or halfhearted job in anything, he lowers the general level of his society and to that extent becomes a burden upon it.

Excellence not only involves competence, of course. It implies also the highest standards and the greatest devotion. Only when we cherish what Whitehead call the "habitual vision of greatness" do our lives find their most satisfying fulfillment. As we make greater demands upon ourselves, we entitle ourselves to look forward to more vitality and greater happiness. Any individual who lives at less than his best cheats himself, and no society that is passive, inert, and preoccupied with its own comforts will long endure.

The idea of quality should never be ignored or forgotten, whether in the most humble activities or in the most exalted places. One of the biggest problems of our present world is that we do not pay enough attention to excellence. For some reason people are crowding toward the bottom levels of life where only the lower prizes are available. Jesus pointed out, and history has proven, that it is the broad road leading toward death that is the most heavily traveled. Many serious problems arise in our lives when our ambitions are aimed below our best.

The ten plagues were sent upon the people of Egypt because their lives lacked quality. The history of our planet, from Cain to the present day, is largely made up of a long series of plagues, famines, pestilence, earthquakes, wars and diseases. We have attracted these to ourselves because we have not lived up to the standards required by the Lord. Even in heaven, people will be happy and compatible according to the measure of the success in that quest.

Thomas Jefferson once pointed out that while life is trying to educate us it is also sorting us. He said, "The geniuses will be raked from the rubbish." Jesus expressed this idea in his parables: the goats being separated from the sheep, the tares being sorted out so that they could be tied in bundles and burned.

The causes for our happiness or unhappiness can be found inside ourselves. To help us develop excellence and achieve [heaven] a divine program has been given to all men. After the dropouts have been eliminated, the rest will be classified according to their degree of excellence. Some of us are like the indolent student whom professor described by saying that he had received great gifts but he had never unwrapped them. What a tragedy when we fail to unwrap the divine gifts of faith, courage, and industry, of which excellence is composed! In developing these traits we must want in capital letters.

Jesus said, "Ask, and it shall be given you; seek, and ye shall find; knock, and it shall be opened unto you." (Matthew 7:7.) We must ask loudly enough, and seek sincerely enough, and knock long enough to get the right answer.

If our desires are weak, our industry will fail and our achievement will be small. There is an old saying that you can't keep a good man down, but that is just not true, some of the potentially best men are presently being kept down by habits of mediocrity, ignorance, sin, sloth, and other natural enemies of excellence. We must turn on enough faith and develop enough ambition to carry us above our present questionable level. We need more excellence in our precepts, more excellence in our motivations, more excellence in our drive, more excellence in our preparation for life, and more excellence in our ambition to live life at its best.

Captain Cook shows us the spirit of excellence when he says about his early-day voyages of discovery, "I had an ambition, not only to go farther than any man had ever been before, but I wanted to go as far as it was possible for any man to go." Suppose that in the journey of our lives we set our goals to go as far as it is possible for anyone to go. Then we would be within reach of the goal of perfection set for us by the Master. We learn perfection by practicing perfection. No excellence is ever developed in a vacuum, and the Lord always fits the back to the burden. If we want a strong back, we should seek out a heavy load. What a thrilling opportunity to dedicate our lives in a quest for excellence.

The sections Taking the Initiative, Circles of Responsibility, and Excellence: An Attribute of Divine-Centered Leaders all focused on the importance of seeking excellence to move from our current state to a more ideal and noble state—a more Christlike state. There is a process which we can follow ourselves and one we can help others follow to bring change and improvement. We call this the repentance process.

Repentance

"We must rise above average. We must rise above mediocrity. We must rise above just getting by. We must do our personal best!"
—Lennon Ledbetter

Our end desire is to become Christlike. The way we do this is by repenting. Repentance is not an act, it is a process—a process of narrowing the gap between our current state and perfection.

Top of the Ladder=Obedience to All the Laws of God=Success

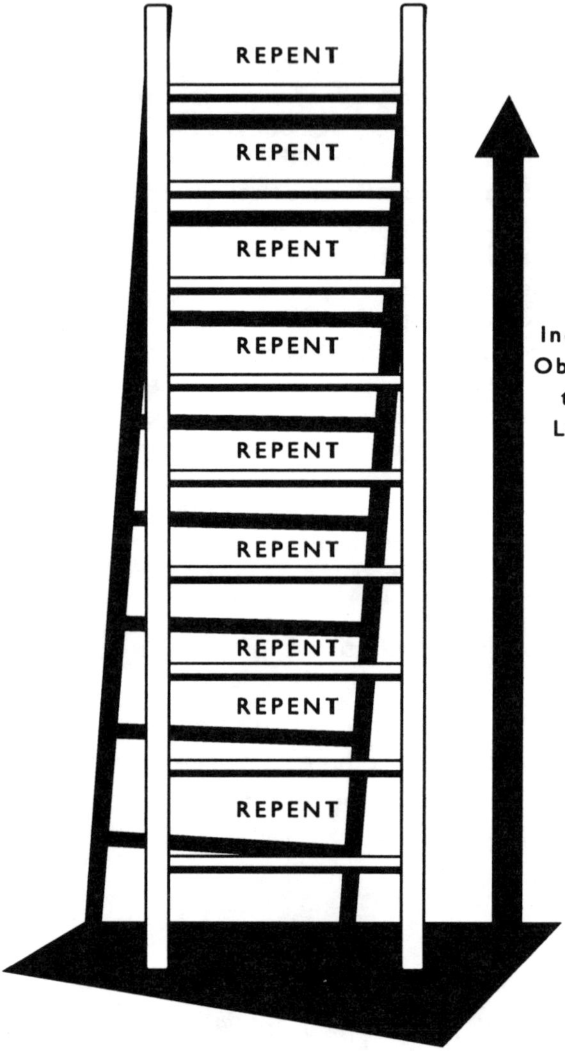

Repentance Ladder

We develop and improve through the repentance process. The process of repentance requires us to learn and live the principles of succss on increasingly higher planes until we are obedient to all the laws of God.

With this perspective, repentance can be viewed as a ladder. "When you climb up a ladder, you must begin at the bottom, and ascend step by step, until you arrive at the top; and so it is with the principles of the Gospel—you must begin with the first, and go on until you learn all the principles of [success]. But it will be a great while after you have passed through the veil before you will have learned them. It is not all to be comprehended in this world; it will be a great work to learn our salvation...even beyond the grave."[17] Repentance is the process of climbing a ladder to perfection and obedience to all the principles of success. We begin the climb in this life and continue toward perfection in the next.

One of the steps of repentance is to never do it again. Forgiveness can only come after we have mastered the command. For if we have truly risen to a level of obedience, we will never commit our former sins. If we do commit former sins, we fall down to a lower rung on the repentance ladder. As we climb the ladder, we can be forgiven for all sins below our current level of obedience. As we repent, we are forgiven of our sins. Christ pays the penalty for ours sins, and we are sanctified (made clean) by the Holy Ghost. As a result of Christ paying the penalty and the Holy Ghost cleansing us, we are made not guilty of those sins. However, we can't be forgiven until we never commit the sin again—until we have truly risen to a higher level of obedience.

Repentance is not an act of going from a sinner to becoming perfectly obedient. We are always sinners, we will never obtain perfect obedience to the laws of God is this life, thus we are always disobedient. Repentance just lessens the level of disobedience. It is the process of becoming more obedient and more Christlike, but we are still sinners. It will be a long time until we are perfect, but we can eventually obtain it through the repentance process.

During the repentance process, our understanding of principles, commandments, and attributes will always exceed the level at which we live them. What we know we should be doing always exceeds what we are actually doing. This fact of life was by design. As a person increases his level of obedience, his knowledge also increases.

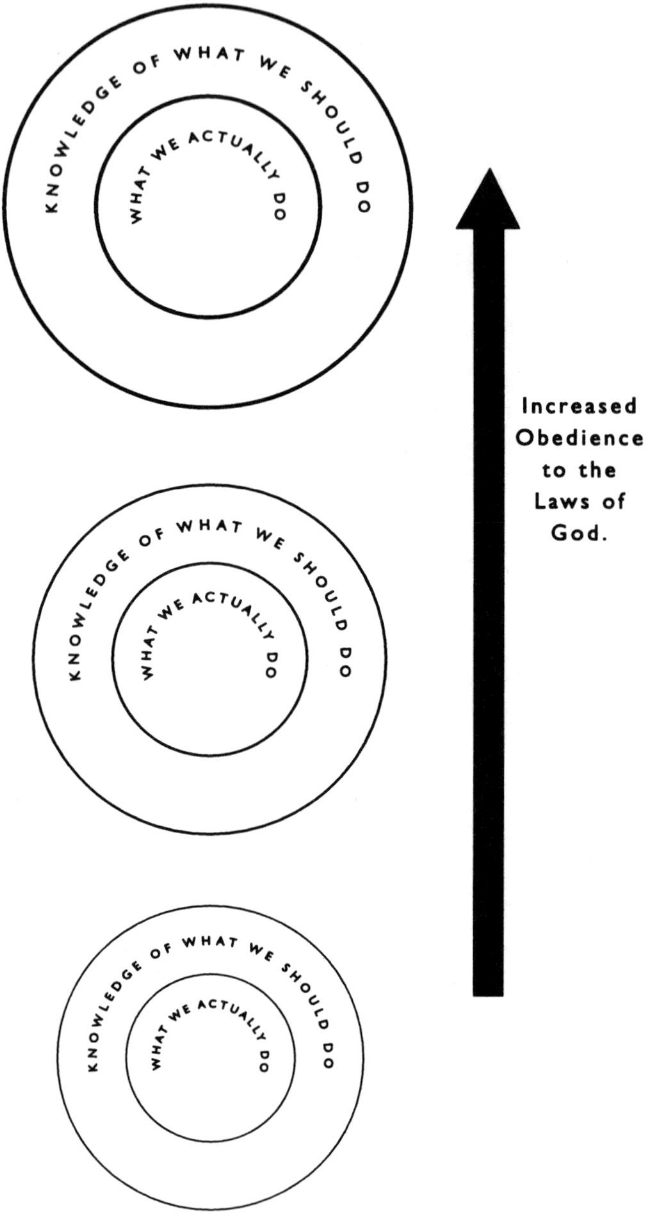

Increased Obedience Circles

Within the repentance process, our understanding of principles will always exceed the level at which we live them. What we know we should do always exceeds what we are actually doing.

"We consider that God has created man with a mind capable of instruction, and a faculty which may be enlarged in proportion to the heed and diligence given to the light communicated from heaven to the intellect; and that the nearer man approaches perfection, the clearer are his views, and the greater his enjoyments, till he has overcome the evils of this life and lost every desire for sin;"[18] God allows us to know more than we are presently living. This allows a person to continually seek improvement without becoming overwhelmed. The model is illustrated on page 71.

God reveals a few of our weaknesses so we can have hope in overcoming them. If he revealed all our inadequacies at once we would be devastated. As we overcome some of our faults, our light grows and we see additional areas that can be improved.[19] Repentance is the process of aligning what we do with what we know. As we begin doing what we know to be right, we will learn more. Then we strive to align our behaviors with the new knowledge we have gained. We continue this process of gaining knowledge and aligning our behavior with that knowledge until we have learned and live in accordance will all the principles of success.

Christ Developed Through Repentance

Some will say that Christ never repented. We disagree. He never sinned, but that does not mean He never used the repentance process. Repentance is the process of progression—the process of becoming perfect. Christ gives us a perfect example of progressing through the repentance process. When Christ was born into mortality, he had a veil placed upon him. Christ was not born with a knowledge of all the principles of success. He had to develop them through gaining knowledge and applying the knowledge he gained. Christ progressed quickly because he was exactly and completely obedient to the knowledge he gained. Because of His obedience He increased in the attributes of godliness until He perfected them all. "And I, John, saw that he received not of the fulness at the first, but received grace for grace; And he received not of the fulness at first, but continued from grace to grace, until he received a fulness."[20]

The greatest hinderment to our progression is sin—not living in accordance with the things we know to be right. Repentance is the process of striving to live in accordance with what we know to be right until we live all the principles of success.

Managing Conflict

"How important it is to know how to disagree without being disagreeable."
—Marvin J. Ashton

The process of Going the Way can result in conflict with others as in Christ cleansing the temple. The following will discuss conflict and how it can be properly managed to produce positive results.

Conflict Defined

Conflict occurs when two or more individuals disagree, clash, or are in opposition to each other with tangible consequences. We often disagree with each other about taste in food or movies, which clothes look best on whom, etc. Basic disagreements become conflicts when the disagreement has tangible consequences—when it affects the way we feel or live. For example, when one person's taste in food differs from those whom he cooks for, conflict occurs when others must eat food they don't enjoy.

Some contend that there is no place for conflict in the gospel of Jesus Christ. They argue that conflict is bad and ought to be avoided. They quote, "he that hath the spirit of contention is not of me, but is of the devil, who is the father of contentions and he stirreth up the hearts of men to contend with anger, one with another."[21] It is not conflict that is bad, but how it is handled. There are two kinds of conflict—conflict that builds and improves people and conflict that destroys. "Contention" and "contending with anger" as mentioned are referring to the destructive conflicts which the devil loves to encourage. Conflict shouldn't be eliminated. When conflict is handled correctly, there are numerous benefits.

Benefits of Conflict

"Problem Awareness: Discussing frustrations identifies poor quality, excessive costs, injustices, and other barriers to effectiveness.

Improved Solutions: Debating opposing views digs into issues, searches for information and insight, and integrates ideas to create solutions responsive to several perspectives.

Productivity: Managed conflict reduces the time wasted by brooding and redoing tasks and results in more efficient use of resources.

Organizational Change: Conflict creates incentives to challenge and change outmoded procedures, assignments, and structures.

Personal Development: Confronting conflict teaches managers and employees how their style affects others and reveals the competencies they need to develop.

Knowledge and Creativity: Elaboration and listening help people retain ideas and understand their implications. They become more creative as they explore alternative and integrate different points of view.

Awareness: Knowing what people are willing to fight about keeps them in touch with each other. People learn what makes themselves and others irritated and angry and what is important to them.

Self-acceptance: Expressing frustrations and important feelings helps people accept and value themselves. Having others listen and respond to their feelings builds people's self-esteem.

Psychological Maturity: Addressing conflicts encourages people to take the perspectives of others and become less egocentric. They feel confident and empowered to cope with difficulties by dealing directly with them.

Morale: Discussion and problem solving help employees release their tensions and stress. They feel confident that they have faced difficulties together and their relationships are strong and open.

Challenge and Fun: The stimulation, arousal, and involvement of conflict can be enjoyable, and can be a welcome break from monotony for employees. It invites people to examine and appreciate intricacies of their relationships."[22]

Causes of Destructive Conflict

"Most conflicts with others extend from conflicts within ourselves. Thus very often, more permanent and powerful means of precluding and resolving destructive conflicts stem from self-confrontation than from confronting others. Doing both can be particularly effective...The true source of virtually all of our conflicts actually resides within us. When we find it, we not only resolve the conflict facing us at the moment; we preclude future conflicts of the same nature from happening again. To explore this exciting, freeing, and wonderful possibility, we must turn within...The underlying key to the preclusion of destructive conflicts is the realization that they ultimately stem from within. Self-understanding is the door to a creative and conflict-free life."[23]

The power to remove destructive conflict comes from within us, although we often try to blame the responsibility of destructive conflict on others. In addition to resolving conflict by changing ourselves, there are three other methods of conflict resolutions. These are discussed in the following excerpts from Conflict-Resolution Strategies.

Responses to Conflict Situations

Excerpts from *Conflict-Resolution Strategies* by Joan A. Stepsis:

Children develop their own personal strategies for dealing with conflict. Even if these preferred approaches do not resolve conflicts successfully, they continue to be used because of a lack of awareness. Conflict-resolution strategies may be classified into three categories—avoidance, diffusion, and confrontation. The accompanying figure demonstrates that avoidance is at one extreme and confrontation is at the other:

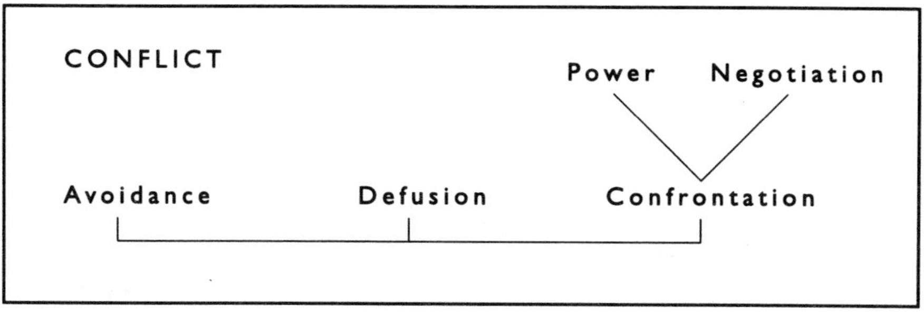

Avoidance

Some people attempt to avoid conflict situations altogether or to avoid certain types of conflict. These people tend to repress emotional reactions, look the other way, or leave the situation entirely (for example, quit a job, leave school, get divorced). Either they cannot face up to such situation effectively, or they do not have the skills to negotiate them effectively.

Although avoidance strategies do have survival value in those instances where escape is possible, they usually do not provide the individual with a high level of satisfaction. They tend to leave doubts and fears about meeting the same type of situation in the future, and about such valued traits as courage or persistence.

Diffusion

This tactic is essentially a delaying action. Diffusion strategies try to cool off the situation, at least temporarily, or to keep the issues so unclear that attempts at confrontation are improbable. Resolving minor points while avoiding or delaying discussion of the major problems, postponing a confrontation until a more auspicious time, and avoiding clarification of the salient issues underlying the conflict are examples of diffusion. Again, as with avoidance strategies, such tactics work when delay is possible, but they typically result in feelings of dissatisfaction, anxiety about the future, and concerns about oneself.

Confrontation

The third major strategy involves an actual confrontation of conflicting issues or persons. Confrontations can further be subdivided into power strategies and negotiation strategies. Power strategies include the use of physical force (a punch in the nose, war); bribery (money, favors); and punishment (withholding love, money). Such tactics are often very effective from the point of view of the "successful" party in the conflict: He wins, the other person loses. Unfortunately, however, for the loser the real conflict may have only just begun. Hostility, anxiety, and actual physical damage are usual byproducts of these win/lose power tactics.

Negotiation Skills

[Although Avoidance, Diffusion, and even Power Confrontations have a valuable role in managing conflict, they all have potentially severe consequences, and frequently fail to solve anything. Probably the best method for managing conflict is in negotiating.]

Successful negotiation, however, requires a set of skills which must be learned and practiced. These skills include 1) the ability to determine the nature of the conflict, 2) effectiveness in initiating confrontations, 3) the ability to hear the other's point of view, and 4) the utilization of problem-solving processes to bring about a consensus.

Diagnosis

Diagnosing the nature of the conflict is the starting point in any attempt at resolution through negotiation. The most important issue which must be decided is whether the conflict is an ideological (value) or a "real" (tangible) conflict—or a combination of both.

Value conflicts are exceedingly difficult to negotiate. If, for example, I believe that women should be treated as equals in every phase of public and private life, and you believe they should be protected or prohibited in certain areas, it would be very difficult for us to come to a position that would satisfy us both.

A difference of values, however, is really significant only when our opposing views affect us in some real or tangible way. If your stand on women's place in society results in my being denied a job that I want and am qualified to perform, then we have a negotiable conflict. Neither of us needs to change his values for us to come to a mutually acceptable resolution of the "real" problem. For example, I may get the job but, in return, agree to accept a lower salary or a different title or not to insist on using the all-male executive dining room. If each of us stands on his principles-maintaining our value conflict—we probably will make little headway. But if, instead, we concentrate on the tangible effects in the conflict, we may be able to devise a realistic solution.

The Israeli-Arab conflict provides a good example of this point. In order to settle the tangible element in the conflict—who gets how much land—ideological differences do not need to be resolved. It is land usage that is the area of conflict amenable to a negotiated settlement.

It is important to determine whether a conflict is a real or a value conflict. If it is a conflict in values resulting in nontangible effects on either party, then it is best tolerated. If, however, a tangible effect exists, that element of the conflict should be resolved.

Initiation

A second skill necessary to conflict resolution is effectiveness in initiating a confrontation. It is important not to begin by attacking or demeaning the opposite party. A defensive reaction in one or both parties usually blocks a quick resolution or differences. The most effective way to confront the other party is for the individual to state the tangible effects the conflict has on him or her. For example: "I have a problem...Due to your stand on hiring women as executives, I am unable to apply for the supervisory position that I feel I am qualified to handle." This approach is more effective than saying, "You male chauvinist pig—you're discriminating against me!" In other words, confrontation is not synonymous with verbal attack.

Listening

After the confrontation has been initiated, the confronter must be capable of hearing the other's point of view. If the initial statement made by the other person is not what the confronter was hoping to hear, defensive rebuttals, a "hard-line" approach, or explanation often follow. Argument-provoking replies should be avoided. The confronter should not attempt to defend himself, explain his position, or make demands or threats. Instead, he must be able to engage in the skill termed reflective or active listening. He should listen and reflect and paraphrase or clarify the other person's stand. When the confronter has interpreted his opposition's position to the satisfaction of the other person, he should again present his own point of view, being careful to avoid value statements and to concentrate on tangible outcomes. Usually, when the confronter listens to the other person, that person lowers his defenses and is, in turn, more ready to hear another point of view. Of course, if both persons are skilled in active listening, the chances of successful negotiating are much enhanced.

Problem-Solving

The final skill necessary to successful negotiation is the use of the problem-solving process to negotiate a consensus decision. The steps in this process are simply stated and easy to apply. (1) Clarifying the problem...What is the tangible issue? Where does each party stand on the issue? (2) Generating and evaluating a number of possible solutions. Often these two aspects should be done separately. First, all possible solutions should be raised in a brainstorming session. Then each proposed solution should be evaluated. (3) Deciding together (not voting) on the best solution. The one solution most acceptable to all parties should be chosen. (4) Planning the implementation of the solution. How will the solution be carried out? When? (5) Finally, planning for an evaluation of the solution after a specified period of time. This last step is essential. The first solution chosen is not always the best or most workable. If the first solution has flaws, the problem-solving process should be begun again at step 1.

We all experience conflict. Many of our conflicts can be resolved through changing ourselves, but even if we are perfect, we will still experience conflict. Jesus was perfect and yet He experienced conflict throughout his life. In addition to changing ourselves, we can also respond to conflict by avoidance, diffusion, or confrontation. The following application suggestion will help us to identify how we manage conflict and identify ways we may be able to manage it better.

Application Ideas for Managing Conflict

The following are scenarios of possible conflicts you may experience. Choose the answer that best describes how you would (not how you should) respond to the situation.

1. You are shopping at Wal-Mart and witness a man leaving the store with unpaid items.
   a. Do nothing.
   b. Rationalize not doing anything by reasoning that he may have a good reason for stealing or maybe I was mistaken and he is not stealing.
   c. Run down the man and make sure he is prosecuted.
   d. Approach the man and seek to understand his situation while yet reproving him for stealing.
   e. None of the above—what would you do?

2. You catch your friend dating someone who is married, and he asks you to keep it a secret.
   a. Let it go, saying nothing.
   b. Talk to your friend at a later time about the incident.
   c. Demand that your friend stop the relationship. If he refuses, you threaten to tell everyone you know.

d. Seek to understand the situation and then make a decision about what ought to be done together.
e. None of the above—what would you do?

3. One of your family members is saying bad things about a good friend of yours.
   a. Do nothing.
   b. Say, "I can see your point but I think so and so is a great person. Maybe you are wrong about them."
   c. Say, "You shouldn't talk about people behind their back and if you every say anything bad about so and so again I will 'Jerry Springer' you."
   d. Discuss with your family member that it is wrong to speak ill of others behind their backs and come to a agreement that they will never speak ill of others around you.
   e. None of the above—what would you do?

4. You are in a relationship where the other person does a particular thing that really bothers you.
   a. Break off the relationship.
   b. Stay in the relationship but never say anything about their actions.
   c. When the person does the thing you don't like, you tell them they have a real problem and need to fix it.
   d. Have a discussion with the person about the problem to help them understand how you feel and how he or she feels about the problem without assigning blame or assuming the other person is wrong.
   e. None of the above—what would you do?

5. Your boss/owner is involved in minor criminal activity with his business.
   a. Quit the job.
   b. Keep the job and subtly express your disapproval but never really do anything about it.
   c. Approach your boss and threaten to report him if he doesn't change his ways.

d. Have a discussion with your boss about how you feel about his actions and come to a resolution together.
e. None of the above—what would you do?

Write the number of answers you had in each of the four responses to see if you have a tendency to follow a particular method of conflict management.

__a=avoidance
__b=diffusion
__c=confrontation-power
__d=confrontation-negotiation

Now answer the question again but this time circle the answer that best represents what Jesus would do. If none of the four options seems to fit what Jesus would do, answer letter e – what would Jesus do?

1. You are shopping at Wal-Mart and witness a man leaving the store with unpaid items.
   a. Do nothing.
   b. Rationalize not doing anything by reasoning that he may have a good reason for stealing or maybe I was mistaken and he is not stealing.
   c. Run down the man and make sure he is prosecuted.
   d. Approach the man and seek to understand his situation while yet reproving him for stealing.
   e. None of the above—what would Jesus do?

2. You catch your friend dating someone who is married, and he asks you to keep it a secret.
   a. Let it go, saying nothing.
   b. Talk to your friend at a later time about the incident.
   c. Demand that your friend stop the relationship. If he refuses, you threaten to tell everyone you know.

   d. Seek to understand the situation and then make a decision about what ought to be done together.
   e. None of the above—what would Jesus do?

3. One of your family members is saying bad things about a good friend of yours.
   a. Do nothing.
   b. Say, "I can see your point but I think so and so is a great person. Maybe you are wrong about them."
   c. Say, "You shouldn't talk about people behind their back and if you every say anything bad about so and so again I will 'Jerry Springer' you."
   d. Discuss with your family member it is wrong to speak ill of others behind their backs and come to a agreement that they will never speak ill of others around you.
   e. None of the above—what would Jesus do?

4. You are in a relationship where the other person does a particular thing that really bothers you.
   a. Break off the relationship.
   b. Stay in the relationship but never say anything about their actions.
   c. When the person does the thing you don't like, you tell them they have a real problem and need to fix it.
   d. Have a discussion with the person about the problem to help them understand how you feel and how he or she feels about the problem without assigning blame or assuming the other person is wrong.
   e. None of the above—what would Jesus do?

5. Your boss/owner is involved in minor criminal activity with his business.
   a. Quit the job.
   b. Keep the job and subtly express your disapproval but never really do anything about it.
   c. Approach your boss and threaten to report him if he doesn't change his ways.

d. Have a discussion with your boss about how you feel about his actions and come to an resolution together.
e. None of the above—what would Jesus do?

Write the number of answers you placed in each of the four responses to see if Jesus has a tendency to follow a particular method of managing conflict.

__a=avoidance
__b=defusion
__c=confrontation-power
__d=confrontation-negotiation

Analyze the difference between what Jesus would do and what you have a tendency to do. Do you need to change how you handle conflict?

Leading By Example

"Live so that others will want to know
Christ because they know you."
—R. Quinn Gardner

In all we do we are constantly influencing the world around us. We are either making it more or less of a heavenly place. We are either influencing those around us to become more Christlike or to become more hellish in nature.

"There is one responsibility which no man can evade; that responsibility is his personal influence. Man's unconscious influence is the silent, subtle radiation of personality—the effect of his words and his actions on others. This radiation is tremendous. Every moment of life man is changing, to degree, the life of the whole world. Every man has an atmosphere which is affecting every other man. He cannot escape for one moment from this radiation of his character, this constant weakening or strengthening of others. Man cannot evade the responsibility by merely saying that it is an unconscious influence. Man can select the qualities he would permit to be radiated. He can cultivate sweetness, calmness, trust, generosity, truth, justice, loyalty, nobility, and make them vitally active in his character. And by these qualities he will constantly affect the world. This radiation, to which I refer, comes from what a person really is, not from what he pretends to be. Every man by his mere living is radiating either sympathy, sorrow, morbidness, cynicism, or happiness and hope or any one of a hundred other qualities. Life is a state of radiation and absorption. To exist is to radiate; to exist is to be the recipient of radiation."[24] Whom we are definitely affects how we lead and influence others.

There are many methods of influence used by leaders. Three levels of influence illustrated on the ladder are what you say, what you do, and who you are. We have all heard the phrase, "do what I say, not what I do." This message has no power to influence others. If we do not do what we say, what we say has no power to motivate or impact others positively. In fact, we will have a negative effect. If we tell people to do things that we do not do ourselves, we become hypocrites and lose the confidence and trust of those whom we seek to lead. What we say is a method of influence, but it is only effective when it is aligned with what we do and who we are. Who we are and our example are prerequisites to influencing others and enable all other methods of influence to become effective.

The second level of influence, "What We Do", is summarized in the statement, "practice what you preach." The things we do have a greater influence on others than the things we say. The greater impact of "what we do"compared to "what we say" is illustrated in the following poem *Sermons We See*, by Edgar Albert Guest:

> I'd rather see a sermon than hear one any day;
> I'd rather one should walk with men than merely tell the way.
> The eye's a better pupil and more willing than the ear,
> Fine counsel is confusing, but example is always clear;
> And the best of all the preachers are the men who live their creeds,
> For to see good put in action is what everybody needs.
> I soon can learn to do it if you'll let me see it done;
> I can watch your hands in action, but your tongue too fast may run.

Ladder of Influence

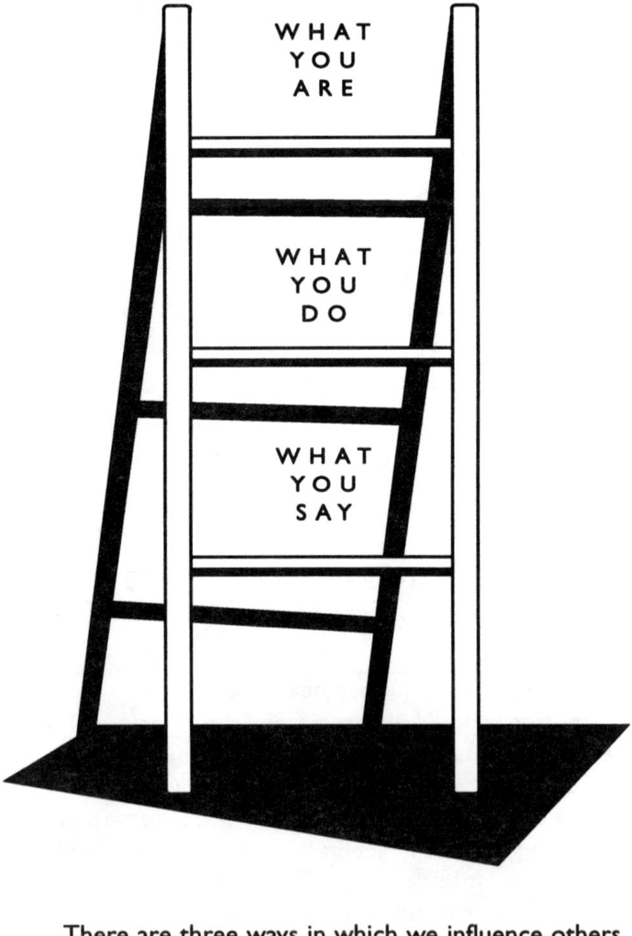

There are three ways in which we influence others.
What we say, what we do, and what we are.

> And the lecture you deliver may be very wise and true,
> But I'd rather get my lessons by observing what you do;
> For I might misunderstand you and the high advice you give,
> But there's no misunderstanding how you act and how you live.

Many would say that rung two, "What You Do," is the highest level of influence, but this is not so, for there are many motives for our actions. If our actions are good but our motivations are bad or dishonorable, our actions will not positively influence others. People can see through our actions to our hearts and it is who we are that impacts them.

The third and highest level of influence is "Who You Are." As Emerson once put it, "What you are shouts so loudly in my ears I cannot hear what you say." To be a Divine-Centered Leader, it is not enough to do what you say and practice what you preach. You must be what you teach. For example, let's consider the principle of service. To operate on the third and highest level of influence, you can't just teach about service or tell others they need to do it. You can't merely go out and do service. You must be a service-oriented person. It must be a part of you. With this paradigm, you view service not as an action you do but as an attribute you possess. Thus, Divine-Centered Leaders do not merely teach about and do service, they are service. From this analysis we see that lasting influence only comes as a result of "Who We Are." Therefore, "What We Say" and "What We Do" are only positive influences if they are in align with "Who We Are."

A mistake some people make is that living a good life is sufficient to influence others for good. As you move up the ladder of influence, you must still do the things on the lower rungs (teaching and doing) to influence others at a higher level. So at level two you don't only do—you do and say; and at the highest level you say, do and are. It is true that people can learn just by observing who we are, but the influence is the greatest when all three methods of influence: teaching, doing, and being, are utilized together.

John C. Maxwell is his book *Developing the Leader Within You* shares the following story of leading by example. "Benjamin

Franklin learned that plaster scattered in the fields would make things grow. He told his neighbors, but they did not believe him. They argued with him, trying to prove that plaster could be of no use at all to grass or grain. After a little while he allowed the matter to drop and said no more about it. Early the next spring Franklin went into the field and sowed some grain. Close to the path, where men would walk, he traced some letters with is finger, put plaster into them, and then sowed seed in the plaster. After a week or two the seed sprang up. As they passed that way, the neighbors were very surprised to see, in brighter green than all the rest of the field, large letters saying, 'This has been plastered.' Benjamin Franklin did not need to argue with his friends anymore about the benefits of plaster for the fields."[25]

Jesus Christ Leads By Example

Jesus perfectly modeled the ability to influence others at the highest level—teaching, doing and being. Jesus taught the way to eternal life, showed it through his life, and actually is the way to eternal life. "Jesus said, 'I am the way, the truth and the life: no man cometh unto the Father but by me.' It is not just that the Son of God brought light into a darkened and fallen world; He is the Light. It is not just that our Savior showed us the way; He is the Way. It is not just that Jesus of Nazareth restored the truth and taught the truth; He is the Truth. We have inherited a Greek notion of truth, one which emphasizes truth as something to be learned, a matter of the head. In fact, the Hebrew notion of truth was something we do and, more precisely, something we are, a matter of the heart. We aren't expected to simply know the truth; we are expected to do the truth and be the truth."[26]

The Three Options of Leaders

What if we find ourselves in a circumstance where we are to lead others to some objective, but we have not obtained the objective or are unable to model it ourselves? We have three options—do nothing, direct to someone else, or personally obtain objectives. Option one ought to almost always be avoided and in most cases we will be most effective in leading others when we lead by the spirit and use a combination of options 2 and 3.

1. *Do Nothing.* We can do nothing and be a leader by position only. We then have nothing to offer our followers for they already posses everything we do. We are not leaders because we have nowhere to take them and nothing to teach. Doing nothing is not an option for Divine-Centered Leaders. If we seek to lead others by ourselves when we do not know the way, we become a blind leader of the blind. In reference to the Pharisees, Jesus taught the results of the blind leading the blind in Matthew 15:14, "they be the blind leaders of the blind. And if blind lead the blind, both shall fall into the ditch." The only time we do nothing is if specifically directed by the spirit to do so.

2. *Direct to Someone Else.* There are many things that we can't do ourselves and our success as leaders often depends on us leading people to others who can do what we can't. We can direct our followers to someone who has the needed knowledge and skills and is willing to teach them. If we earnestly seek His counsel, the Spirit will help us know who and when to direct to someone else.

3. *Personally Obtain Objective.* As was stated in the first chapter, personal success precedes success with others. As we personally obtain objectives, we put ourselves in a position to lead others along the path we have taken. We can spend the time and effort to obtain the necessary knowledge and skills. If we prayerfully ask, the Spirit will help us in this endeavor.

An Example of the Three Options

Scenario—my dad wants to teach me to how to play the trumpet, but is unable to play the trumpet himself.

1. *Do Nothing.* My dad could try to teach me himself but he would have nothing to teach me because we are both on the same plane—neither of us can play the trumpet.
2. *Direct to Someone Else.* My dad could direct me to someone who can play the trumpet and they could teach me.
3. *Personally Obtain Objectives.* My dad could first learn to play the trumpet and then he could teach me.

Leading by the Spirit

"Where true saints are concerned, they excel all others in knowledge and wisdom because they have the mind of Christ; they are taught from on high by the Spirit."
—Bruce R. McConkie

The Spirit is the greatest resource leaders have to tap into. The Spirit knows all things, can teach us all things, and can help us teach others all things. As we lead by the Spirit, we will lead as Christ leads for the Spirit and Christ are one. As we lead by the Spirit, we are doing and saying the things Christ would do and say and we will know others as Christ knows them. As we lead by the Spirit, our abilities become unlimited because the abilities of the Spirit are unlimited.

Of all the gifts we can enjoy, of all the characteristics we can possess, of all the skills we can obtain, this gift of the Spirit stands paramount in our efforts to become Christlike leaders. The disciples on the American continent understood this concept well. We read that "they did pray for that which they most desired; and they desired that the Holy Ghost should be given unto them."[27] These disciples understood that with the guidance and direction of the Holy Ghost, it is possible to be able to say and do what Christ would do if He were present on the earth today.

As we seek to become Divine-Centered Leaders, we too must desire above all things to have the Spirit of the Lord with us. As we live worthily and obtain this gift, we will understand more fully how to lead like Christ did. We will know the steps needed to develop the characteristics that Christ possessed. We will have the strength to allow the Lord to slowly mold us into the people He wants us to become. Truly, if we seek to become like Jesus Christ, it is His spirit we should seek to obtain. "For they that are wise and . . . have taken the Holy Spirit for their guide... the Lord shall be in their midst, and his glory shall be upon them..."[28]

Since the spirt is the greatest resource we have, how do we obtain it and lead by it? First, we must be humble. We must seek the will of the Lord through his spirit and seek to lead His people as He wants them lead. Humility is a prerequisite to leading by the spirit because the proud are so caught up in their "own" knowledge and brilliance that they will not listen to God's voice. Humility is an acknowledged recognition of our dependence on a higher power. Divine-Centered Leaders will never succeed unless they have the spirit of humility for without humility we cannot tap into the spirit which is the only source of power and strength.

Marion G. Romney says, "If you want to obtain and keep the guidance of the spirit, you can do so by following this simple four-point program. One, pray. Pray diligently. Pray with each other. Pray in public in the proper places. Learn to talk to the Lord; call upon his name in great faith and confidence. Second, study and learn the gospel. Third, live righteously; repent of your sins by confessing them and forsaking them. Then conform to the teachings of the gospel. Fourth, give service in the Church. If you will do these things, you will get the guidance of the Holy Spirit and you will go through this world successfully, regardless of what the people of the world say or do"[29]

Application Ideas for Leading by the Spirit

Using Marion G. Romney's formula for obtaining the Spirit, use the following chart to evaluate your current behavior in each of the four areas. Identify weaknesses you have, and then look for ways to overcome them.

Application Table for Leading by the Spirit

	Weakness	Ways to Improve
PRAYER		
LEARNING & STUDYING THE SCRIPTURES		
LIVING RIGHTEOUSLY (BEING HUMBLE)		
SERVICE		

Intergrity

"When one is loyal to the truth, we say he is a person of integrity. When one is loyal to the truth under intense opposition, we say he is a person of great integrity."
—Royden G. Derrick

In order to Go the Way and lead by the spirit, we must be people of integrity. Integrity is commonly defined as a state of being whole, entire, or undiminished. This definition implies an undeviating commitment to a set of values, principles, or beliefs. This type of commitment is demonstrated throughout history by great men and women. In the Bible, Daniel illustrates this type of integrity when he refuses King Nebuchadnezzar's command for him to partake of meat and strong drink, and then again when he continues to pray to God daily, despite the new law to worship only King Belshazzar. Even when threatened with punishment of the lion's den, Daniel refused to act contrary to what he knew to be true. Job also exhibited integrity. Even though Job experienced all manner of suffering, affliction, and pain, he refused to compromise his faith and commitment to God. When tempted to curse God, Job said, "...till I die I will not remove mine integrity from me. My righteousness I hold fast, and will not let go; my heart shall not reproach me so long as I live."[30]

Although completeness is a vital characteristic of integrity, Christlike integrity must be more than simply being whole or undivided. The Random House Dictionary defines integrity as "soundness of and adherence to moral principle and character; uprightness; honesty." Surely Satan is an individual of absolute commitment. He is the father of all lies and is determined that each of us will be miserable like he is. He never strays from this path of destruction.

Satan may be committed, but he has refused to be committed to truth. His decision to follow another path has not changed the truth. Truth is constant. It is up to each of us to decide whether or not we will accept truth and live by it. In John 8:32 Christ teaches,

High Integrity

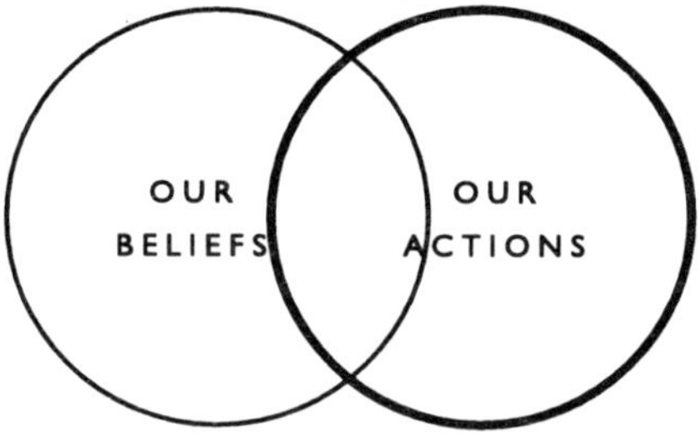

Low Integrity

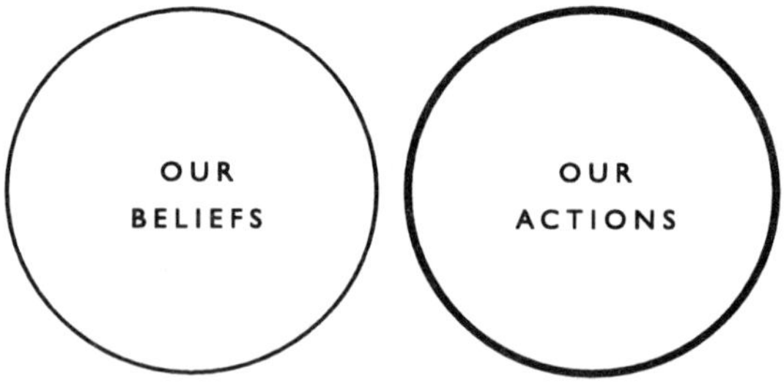

No Integrity

The Integrity Circles

If we were to view our lives as two circles, with one representing our beliefs, and the other circle representing our actions, how close would these two circles be?

"And ye shall know the truth and the truth shall make you free." Like Satan, when we choose to live by principles other than truth, we are tricking ourselves into living in bondage.

Christ has taught, "If ye know these things, happy are ye if ye do them."[31] True happiness then, as well as our eventual salvation, will come as a result of our determination to find truth and to live by it. If we are committed to anything but the principles of truth, we will ultimately be unsuccessful as leaders, parents, and individuals.

Hypocrisy is the opposite of integrity. The Savior frequently chastised hypocrites in the scriptures. Hypocrisy is basically an incongruency between what one believes and how one lives. This inconsistency between ones beliefs and ones actions shows an obvious lack of integrity. Each of us is guilty of this inconsistency to one degree or another. If we were to view our lives as two circles, with one circle representing our beliefs and the other circle representing our actions, how close would these two circles be? Would the two circles be touching or would they be far apart? The closer our circles become, the more closely our actions reflect our beliefs, and the more integrity we have.

Why is it that we believe in high and lofty principles and yet don't live in accordance with them? Ghandi has said, "there are 999 who believe in honesty for every honest man." What makes integrity elusive to so many? How can we live with integrity?

One of the factors that persuades us to violate principles we believe to be true is the flesh—our physical bodies. The flesh does not seek to live in accordance with correct principles such as honesty. The flesh doesn't distinguish between right and wrong. The flesh's only desire is to obtain pleasure and avoid pain. Thus, if we follow the desire of the flesh, we will violate Eternal principles. We will violate the principles of success. The way we can align our life with the principles of success is by following the light of Christ or our conscience.

Stephen Robinson explains the nature of the physical body and the spirit body as follows, "[the physical body] naturally seeks pleasure rather than righteousness because it has no ability to distinguish between right and wrong—flesh has no conscience. I mean that literally. Just as a thermometer cannot detect radiation and a Geiger counter cannot detect heat, so our flesh cannot detect light and truth—it wasn't designed to do it. Flesh can distinguish only between pleasure and pain, between "feels good" and "doesn't feel good," and therefore it urges us to act upon that distinction alone. The unredeemed carnal self, our flesh and its desires, readily serves the devil because it has no moral sense, no spiritual discernment, and no conscience. It was not designed that way—the ability to make those distinctions was given to our spirit, our flesh is morally blind and is therefore an enemy to God, for Satan can successfully argue to the flesh that sin is pleasurable even when he can't successfully argue to the spirit that sin is right. Consequently, being both incredibly powerful and morally blind, until and unless the carnal self yields to the enticing of the Holy Spirit and accepts the leadership of our own spirit with its moral vision, it remains a loose cannon and an enemy to God.[32] But please note that we do not seek to destroy or escape the flesh or carnal self but rather to subject it to the Spirit and to sanctify it. The capacity for pleasure is not, after all, evil. It is necessary and desirable—not when it is our highest priority but rather when it accepts the leadership of the Spirit and serves the interests of the Spirit."[33]

When we are faced with choices, we are pulled by two forces—the light of Christ and the flesh. The key to developing integrity is to adhere to our conscience or the light of Christ. Our conscience tells us what is right and wrong; what we should and should not do. As we adhere to the direction we receive from our conscience, we align our actions with the principles of success. The ability to listen to and adhere to our conscience, or the light of Christ, is a developed talent. We often do not listen to or adhere to our conscience as a result of justification and rationalization. Spencer Kimball has said, "Practically all dishonesty owes its continued existence and growth to this inward distortion we call 'self-justification.' It is the first, the worst and most insidious and damaging form of cheating—cheating ourselves."[34]

Stephen R. Covey teaches how rationalization can result in us not following our conscience. "When we hear the first whispering of conscience, we do one of two things—we either act in harmony with it, or we immediately begin to rationalize—tell ourselves 'rational lies'—as to why we should make some other choice. If we choose the first response, we feel peaceful. We create alignment with true north. We grow in our ability to recognize that inner voice and in our personal effectiveness. If we choose the second option, we feel disharmony and tension. The key to acting with integrity is to simply stop playing the game. Learn to listen—as well as to conscience, to our own response. The instant we feel ourselves saying, "Yes, but" change it to, "Yes, and." No rationalizing. No justifying. Just do it. Look at every expression of conscience as an invitation to create greater alignment with the fundamental Laws of Life. Then listen, respond…listen, respond. In their deep inner lives, they know what they ought to be doing. And they know it would improve quality of life. The challenge is to develop the character and competence to listen to it and live by it—to act with integrity in the moment of choice."[35]

Why do we seek to justify and rationalize actions that violate our conscience? Because the flesh persuades us to make decisions based on pleasure and pain instead of right and wrong. For example, you make a mistake at work that costs the company thousands of dollars, which could never be traced to you, and then your boss asks you if you know anything about it. Your conscience tells you to tell the truth because it is the right thing to do. Your flesh tells you to lie to avoid the pain and punishment that may be associated with taking responsibility for the mistake. When we receive direction from the light of Christ, we often rationalize or justify why we should follow the desires of the flesh, our personal desires, or our own wisdom and rationale.

While I (Cameron) was serving a mission in Hawaii, I fell into the trap of rationalizing to the point of not adhering to the Holy Ghost. While I was serving as a mission leader, I was laboring with another missionary, Aaron Kelly. We went to an appointment to teach a man, Todd, the gospel. We taught for about an hour, and it went fairly smoothly. The Spirit was strong, but Todd didn't seem to respond to the Spirit. After the discussion, Todd began to ask anti-Christian questions. He was very knowledgeable of Christianity. He knew the scriptures better than a lot of missionaries. He was the master of deceit. He was skilled in twisting our words and using analogies and stories to justify his false doctrines. I have never met a more cunning and deceiving man. He acted as if he was interested in learning, but was doing everything he could to prove us wrong.

I would describe Todd as follows. Todd went about declaring to the people that there was no gospel of Jesus Christ. He preached many things that were flattering to the people; and this he did that he might overthrow the doctrine of Christ. And he labored diligently that he might overthrow the doctrine of Christ. And he labored diligently that he might lead away many hearts; and he sought much opportunity that he might come unto me. And he was learned and had a perfect knowledge of the language; therefore, he could use much flattery and much power of the devil. And he hoped to shake us from our faith.

Todd had led many people away from Christianity. Todd's real intent was to prove us wrong and lead us away from Christ, but this fact was not found out until a later visit by other missionaries. During our first meeting, Aaron Kelly and I didn't know his real intent. He put on a good act—acting as if he really wanted to learn about Christ.

After we had taught him for about an hour, Todd began to ask anti-Christian questions. Elder Kelly and I continually directed Todd to prayer and taught him that prayer would be how he would find out if what we said was true. After this went on for a while, Todd said, " I will pray with you. I will pray with you right now." Todd said he would pray that if we taught the truth then one of us would die immediately. So, if he prayed and one of us died then he would know that what we taught was true. We replied by saying that answers to our prayers do not come via signs and wonders but by the Holy Ghost. Todd continued to say he was going to pray for one of us to die, and he said that we were scared and that is why we didn't want him to pray. We replied by saying that we were not afraid. We didn't want him to pray for us to die because that is not how prayers are answered.

After we had discussed this issue a while, Todd began to demand a sign. He said, "unless you show me a sign I will not believe." At this point I was filled with the Holy Spirit. It rushed into my body filling me from my head to my toes—it was an all encompassing, powerful feeling. I could feel the power of God within me. And words from the Spirit clearly flowed into my head saying "strike the man dumb, this will be his sign." The message was clear. I knew what I was to say and do and there was no doubt in my mind that when I spoke Todd would be struck dumb. I have never at anytime felt the power and Spirit of God so strongly, but instead of acting upon the prompting of the Spirit I began to rationalize why I should not act upon the direction of the Spirit. I recalled the accounts in the scriptures when individuals were struck dumb and they died. I had never killed any man and I was hesitant to do so. I knew if I were to strike him dumb, he would be damned and have no chance to change. I rationalized that I wanted to help him change and accept the gospel; not damn and condemn him. He had acted as if he was interested, and I thought there may still be some way we could get him to accept the gospel. Todd continued to demand a sign over and over again and Aaron Kelly continued to talk with him. Then, the second time, the Spirit rushed into my body again and told me to strike the man dumb. I continued with my rationalizing and shrunk that I would not have to destroy this man. Then the third time the Spirit came to me and said, "strike the man dumb," and again I failed to act upon it.

I failed to act upon the promptings of the Holy Spirit because of my rationalization. This experience weighed heavily upon me for months. I knew I should have struck him dumb as the Spirit directed me, and I felt great guilt and remorse. The Lord tried to use me as an instrument but I didn't follow the direction I received. As I sought repentance for my sin, it was revealed to me what would have happened had I struck Todd dumb and the results of my disobedience. The Lord revealed to me that Todd was never going to change and that the only way he could have been stopped from leading people away from Christ was to be struck dumb. And that because I didn't strike him dumb, he continued to lead people astray. Had I struck him dumb, many who followed him would have been brought to a knowledge of the fullness of the gospel and many others who heard of him being struck dumb would have been brought to Christ. Striking Todd dumb would have resulted in his destruction, but would have also resulted in many people coming to Christ and joining His church. As I repented, I felt the weight of each soul that could have been saved but was not because I failed to adhere to the Spirit. Even as I write this experience now, I feel great pain, remorse, and sorrow for the souls I could have helped to save.

Eventually, I received forgiveness from the Lord, but not until I experienced great pain. Following this experience, I was determined to follow the prompting of the Spirit no matter what, without question, and without rationalizing. I share this experience because it clearly shows the effects of following or not following the Spirit. Often times we don't see or understand the full effects of following or not following the Spirit, but you can be positive that failure to hear or failure to follow the Spirit when heard will be extremely damaging, while adhering to the Spirit will always bring blessings. We all receive promptings from the Holy Ghost and direction from the light of Christ. It is vital to our happiness and the happiness of others that we learn to hear and adhere to these promptings. There is no reason great enough to justify not following the Spirit.

Many people will justify violating principles of success for material gains. Money acquired through the violation of principles is never worth its cost. "For what is a man profited, if he shall gain the whole world, and lose his own soul? Or what shall a man give in exchange for his soul?"[36] Money obtained through the violation of principles is what the scriptures refer to as filthy lucre. "Filthy lucre is blood money—it is that which is obtained by stealing. Filthy lucre is that which comes through robbery or through gambling. It is that which might be had through sin or sinful operations. Filthy lucre is that which might come from the sale of liquor, wines, and beer. It is that which comes from bribery or from exploitation. I believe that unearned money or compromise money is filthy. Graft money is tainted and that which comes through deceptions, excessive charges, oppression to the poor. Men who accept wages, salaries, or fees who do not give commensurate time, energy, devotion, or service collect money that is not as clean as it should be...Is money taken on the Sabbath, when it is unnecessary, unclean money?"[37] We must guard against the temptation to go against what we know to be right—to compromise our integrity—for money or the gain of worldly possessions.

What counsel/direction should we be loyal to? Where is your loyalty? God or man? Often we seek to please those around us or participate in actions we know to be wrong because we don't want to offend or displease those around us. When faced with decisions that involve social pressure, we need to decide if we are going to follow the commands of the Lord or the counsel of men. Peter gives us a shining example of integrity in the midst of opposition from others. Peter would stand with boldness and strength before magistrates and rulers who could imprison him, flog him, and perhaps even take his life. On one occasion when brought before the high priest to be questioned why he had violated their command not to preach, "Peter and the other apostles answered and said, We ought to obey God rather than men."[38]

Another common rationalization is that it is okay to violate what we know to be right for small things or things of lesser importance. Howard W. Hunter taught, "There are some who will admit it is morally wrong to be dishonest in big things yet believe it is excusable if they are of lesser importance. Is there any difference between dishonesty involving a thousand dollars or that which involves only a dime? Is there any difference in principle between a little white lie and the perjury of a witness in a court of law or in a congressional investigation committee under oath? Are there really degrees of dishonesty, depending upon whether or not the subject is great or small?"[39]

It is often the small or seemingly unimportant violations of our conscience that can be most damaging. Every choice we make affects our character, our inner self, who we are. "Every time you make a choice you are turning the central part of you, the part of you that chooses, into something a little different from what it was before. And taking your life as a whole, with all your innumerable choices, all your life long you are slowly turning this central thing either into a heavenly creature or into a hellish creature: either into a creature that is in harmony with God, and with other creatures, and with itself, or else into one that is in a state of war and hatred with God, and with its fellow-creatures, and with itself. To be the one kind of creature is heaven: that is, it is joy and peace and knowledge and power. To be the other means madness, horror, idiocy, rage, impotence, and eternal loneliness. Each of us at each moment is progressing to the one state or the other."[40]

Acting with integrity—doing what we believe to be right—is essential to leadership and the leadership process. In fact, acting with integrity (adhering to conscience) is how we become leaders. For "people do not become leaders through striving to be leaders; rather, they become leaders through striving to live in harmony with what is right." (Robert Millet)

Application Ideas for Integrity

1. Seek to listen to the light of Christ (conscience) and avoid rationalization. As you begin to analyze how you adhere to your conscience, you will see that when you receive direction from your conscience or the Spirit, you may have a tendency to respond by saying "yes, but" and rationalize why you should do something else. Seek to change your response from "yes, but" to "yes", and act upon it. Make a conscious effort to make decisions based upon your conscience and the Spirit without rationalizing.

2. Choose one or two principles you believe in (service, hard work, exercise, effective time management, honesty, etc). During the week, evaluate how closely you live these principles. At the end of

each day, stop to evaluate what you did that supported your chosen belief. Were there actions that contradicted this belief? What can you do to live this principle more effectively the following day?

Integrity Table

My Belief		
Actions today thatsupport my belief		
Actions today contradicting my belief		
How can I live this principle better tomorrow?		

Living a Balanced Life

"If a man does not blend into his life a program of self-improvement to bring about a sensible balance, he no doubt will end up a failure."
—John H. Vandenberg

Christ is the perfect example of being well developed in all facets of life. He began at a young age to become diversified and sought perfection in all aspects of His life. Luke's description of the development of young Jesus illustrates this point. "And Jesus increased in wisdom [intellectual], and stature [physical], and in favour with God [spiritual] and man [social]."[41]

Divine-Centered Leaders model Christ's example of living a balanced life. Our lives and our needs are multidimensional. They can be divided into four categories: spiritual, social, intellectual, and physical. Divine-Centered Leaders are well-developed in all four areas. The four areas are interrelated like the four tires of an automobile. If one tire is low on air, the other three are adversely affected. If one tire goes completely flat, the other three tires are unable to function. Can you say one tire on a car is more important than another? Of course not. So it is with the four elements of our life (spiritual, social, intellectual, and physical)—one is not more important than another. We cannot say our spiritual development is the most important or that our social development is the most important. For success in one area requires success in the other areas. The four areas of our lives are highly interrelated. In fact, you could say that everything we do is spiritual; for all our social, intellectual and physical activities affect our spirituality.

As said the Lord, "Wherefore, verily I say unto you that all things unto me are spiritual, and not at any time have I given unto you a law which was temporal: neither any man, nor the children of men; neither Adam, your father, whom I created."[42] The four areas of our lives are more closely related than most people think. For example, our spirituality is effected by our physical health a great deal more than most people realize. There is a close relationship between physical and spiritual well-being. If your physical health is impaired, your spirituality will also suffer. We perform at our best when there is a balance between the four areas.

Brigham Young taught the value of developing all aspects of our lives and the need and benefits of living a diversified life:

"Our work, our every-day labor, our whole lives are within the scope of our religion. This is what we believe and what we try to practice. Yet the Lord permits a great many things that he never commands. I have frequently heard my old brethren in the Christian world make remarks about the impropriety of indulging in pastimes and amusements. The Lord never commanded me to dance, yet I have danced: you all know it, for my life is before the world. Yet while the Lord has never commanded me to do it, he has permitted it. I do not know that he ever commanded the boys to go and play at ball, yet he permits it. I am not aware that he ever commanded us to build a theater, but he has permitted it, and I can give the reason why. Recreation and diversion are as necessary to our well-being as the more serious pursuits of life. There is not a man in the world but what, if kept at any one branch of business or study, will become like a machine. Our pursuits should be so diversified as to develop every trait of character and diversity of talent. If you would develop every power and faculty possessed by your children, they must have the privilege of engaging in and enjoying a diversity of amusements and studies;"[43]

Application Idea for Living a Balanced Life

1. Complete "Balanced Life Evaluation Form" in the Appendix on page 165.

PART 5

Showing the Way

STEP 3: ***Showing the Way***
Leading Others to Success

STEP 2: ***Going the Way***
Leading by Example, Being a Person of Intergrity

STEP 1: ***Knowing the Way***
Having Vison, Providing Direction and Purpose

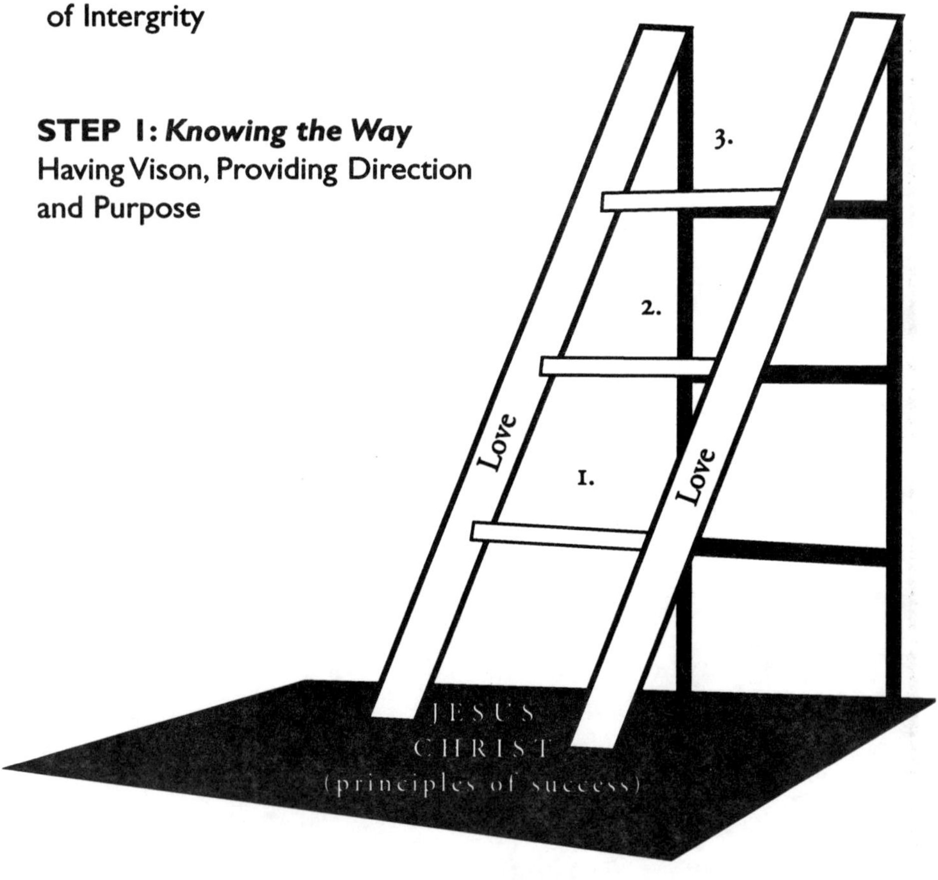

"It is upon the rock of our Redeemer who is Christ the Son of God that ye must build your foundation."

PART 5: SHOWING THE WAY

"True shepherds nourish and care for each member of the flock and keep them in remembrance. They do not simply number them. Shepherds know and care for their flock. A shepherd cannot rest when even one of the flock is lost."
—Robert D. Hales

"Coaching isn't an addition to a leader's job, it's an integral part of it."
—George S. Odiorne

Showing the Way is where the change and growth of others takes place. Let's say you are great at the elements classified as Knowing the Way and Going the Way, yet fail at the elements of Showing the Way to others. Are you a leader? No. In addition to effectively setting vision and purpose and obtaining personal successes, leaders must enable their followers to obtain goals. People may be successful, but they are not leaders until they make others successful as well.

"Divine-Centered Leaders Show the Way by recognizing that each human being has the potential to become like Christ and helping others to see this divine potential. They recognize that each person has different talents and abilities and values these differences. They demonstrate friendship, love, and concern for each individual within their influence. They ensure that people are their highest priority and place people before projects and things. They cultivate loving relationships and communicate effectively with others."[1]

Divine-Centered Leaders Show the Way by putting the needs of others first and their own needs second. "They willingly sacrifice to be a servant and steward to those they lead. They patiently teach their followers correct principles. They allow followers the freedom to choose their actions. Then, with compassion balanced by justice, hold them accountable for the consequences. They clearly communicate the expectations of each follower in accordance with his own potential. They work diligently to teach, train, and prepare others to lead as Christ lead."[2]

What is Our Potential?

"You can count how many seeds are in an apple, but can you count how many apples are in a seed?"
—Lennon Ledbetter

What is our greatest potential? Is it not to become like God? Christ has told us of our divine potential. Christ said in Psalms 82:3, "Ye are gods; and all of you are children of the most high." And in Matthew 5:48 the Lord commands us to "be ye therefore perfect, even as your Father which is in heaven is perfect." We each have the potential to become like God—to obtain all the joy and possessions which God now enjoys.

C. S. Lewis provides us with additional insight into our divine potential: "The command Be ye perfect is not idealistic gas. Nor is it a command to do the impossible. He is going to make us into creatures that can obey that command. He said (in the Bible) that we were 'gods' and He is going to make good His words. If we let Him—for we can prevent Him, if we choose—He will make the feeblest and filthiest of us into a god or goddess, a dazzling, radiant, immortal creature, pulsating all through with such energy and joy and wisdom and love as we cannot now imagine, a bright stainless mirror which reflects back to God perfectly (though, of course, on a smaller scale) His own boundless power and delight and goodness. The process will be long and in parts very painful; but that is what we are in for. Nothing less. He meant what He said."[3]

We Must Seek to Obtain Our Potential

The first step to becoming like God is believing in it. Then we must perform to our greatest potential. There are many obstacles blocking the attainment of our full potential. "Frequently people are ashamed to be outstanding. It seems so much more comfortable to be mediocre. There is constant pressure pushing people toward being average, and when one has average goals and average ambitions, excellence becomes very difficult to achieve. Satan is the inventor of an unprofitable state of satisfaction that makes peoples content in just getting by."[4]

Feelings of apathy and satisfaction often result in people performing far below their potential. "The greatest waste in the world is not the devastation of war; it is not the cost of crime; it is not the erosion of our soils; nor is it the depletion of our raw materials, nor the loss of our gold supply. The greatest waste in the world is that human beings, you and I, live so far below the level of our possibilities. Compared with what we might be, we are just partly alive."[5]

We must continually strive for excellence if we are to obtain the greatest that is within us.

How Understanding Divinity Affects How We View Others

As we understand our potential and the potential of others, we will act differently. We will treat ourselves and others differently. Divine-Centered Leaders accept people as they are but treat them as they can become. We should treat all those we associate with as we would treat Christ, for that is their potential—to become like Christ, full of glory and perfection.

C. S. Lewis provides us with insight on the divine potential of all beings: "The load, or weight, or burden of my neighbor's glory should be laid on my back, a load so heavy that only humility can carry it, and the backs of the proud will be broken. It is a serious thing to live in a society of possible gods and goddesses, to remember that the dullest and most uninteresting person you can talk to may one day be a creature which, if you say it now, you would be strongly tempted to worship, or else a horror and a corruption such as you now meet, if at all, only in a nightmare. All day long we are, in some degree, helping each other to one or other of these destinations. It is in the light of these overwhelming possibilities, it is with the awe and the circumspection proper to them, that we should conduct all our dealings with another, all friendships, all loves, all play, all politics. There are no ordinary people. You have never talked to a mere mortal...it is immortals whom we joke with, work with, marry, snob and exploit...Next to the blessed sacrament itself, your neighbor is the holiest object presented to your senses."[6]

All beings we interact with are full of divine potential, but we must first realize this potential before we can help them attain it. It is vital to our success as leaders that we understand what others can become because our interaction with others either helps them toward or away from their divine potential.

Helping Others See Their Potential

Divine-Centered Leaders help others recognize and work toward their full potential.

To affirm the potential of others, we must view them with an eye of faith, seeing their potential instead of their present status. If we truly believe in Jesus Christ, we will also believe in the unseen identity and potential of our Heavenly Father's children. We will see no ordinary people, but gods and goddesses and treat them all accordingly. We don't treat them in terms of their behavior, but rather in terms of their potential, of what they can become. Goethe put it this way, "Treat a man as he is and he will remain as he is; treat a man as he can and should be and he will become as he can and should be."[7] As we treat people as they can and should be, we help them to progress. We help them to move from where they currently are to a more Christlike life.

Of the religious leader Joseph Smith, one writer said, "He could take an ordinary man and place the mirror of his potential greatness before him and then have that man re-channel his life's energy for the remainder of his life on the new vision. This transformation is a divine manifestation which would not be ignored by anyone . . . Whenever such an awakening of a man occurs, religious people say, 'God is in this place.'"

As we help others recognize their divine potential, we will awaken in them a drive to excel, a desire to obtain their potential, and a hope for the wondrous life which will occur when perfection and eternal life are achieved.

To truly Show the Way to others, we must see their potential and understand that each person is different and unique and value that difference.

Diversity

"Our ability to reach unity in diversity will be the beauty and test of our civilization."
—Mahatma Gandhi

Each of us is different and unique. We all have different talents, gifts, and skills. We have all had different experiences which affect how we see and act within the world. Diversity is a result of differences. Many view differences as a negative because it can lead to conflict which, if handled poorly, results in strife, hatred, contention, destruction and division. If differences or conflicts are handled correctly, they can strengthen relationships, build love and trust, improve decisions, bring out the greatest power within people, and cultivate unity. It is possible to have unity and diversity. We see this exhibited all throughout nature. "In nature we may observe both a unity and a diversity. Though a given species of grass may have general characteristics in which all the varieties of grasses are alike, yet men have not yet found two blades of grass precisely alike. In all the leaves of the forest, there have not yet been found two leaves exactly alike; among all the hordes of men—the millions living and the millions dead—no two have yet been found one of which is a precise counterpart of the other. It is so everywhere you look in nature; in animal or plant life; in mountains, rivers or valleys; in the sands or among the shells of the sea shore—everywhere unity of kind, of groups, but infinite variety of individuals."[8]

The key to benefitting from diversity is to value the mental, emotional, and psychological differences between people. And the key to valuing those differences is to realize that all people see the world not as it is, but as they are. A person who is a truly effective leader has the humility to recognize his own perceptual limitations and to appreciate the rich resources available through interaction with the hearts and minds of other human beings. That person values the differences because they add to his knowledge and to his understanding of reality. When we're left to our own experiences, we constantly suffer from a shortage of data.

Is it possible for two people to disagree and both be right? Yes. For example, in a room the temperature is 70 degrees and one individual says it is cold while the other says it is hot. Is the room hot or is the room cold? Which of the two individuals is right? Does one have to be right and one wrong? No, both are right from their perspective. It would be silly for the individual that was hot to tell the person who said it was cold that he was wrong or stupid because he thought it is cold. Unless we value the differences in our perceptions, unless we value each other and give credence to the possibility that we're both right, that life is not always a dichotomous either/or, that there are almost always third alternatives, we will never be able to transcend the limits of that conditioning.

When we become aware of someone whose perceptions are different from ours we should say, "Good! You see it differently! Help me see what you see." If two people have the same opinion, one is unnecessary. It's not going to do any good for two people with the same opinion to communicate with each other other than to affirm and support their ideas. We increase our awareness and understanding by speaking with people who perceive things differently than us.[9]

The Lord understands the value of diversity and has set up a system in which all individuals are different; possessing different talents, skills, and gifts. Christ made us different so we could teach one another. Each individual is different, yet the group as a whole is unified. This is explained in 1 Corinthians 12:4-27:

> "Now there are diversities of gifts, but the same Spirit. And there are differences of administrations, but the same Lord. And there are diversities of operations, but it is the same God which worketh all in all.
>
> "But the manifestation of the Spirit is given to every man to profit withal. For to one is given by the Spirit the word of wisdom; to another the word of knowledge by the same Spirit; To another faith by the same Spirit; to another the gifts of healing by the same Spirit; To another the working of miracles; to another prophecy; to another discerning of spirits; to another [divers] kinds of tongues; to another the interpretation of tongues:
>
> "But all these worketh that one and the selfsame Spirit, dividing to every man severally as he will. For as the body is one, and hath many members, and

all the members of that one body, being many, are one body: so also [is] Christ. For by one Spirit are we all baptized into one body, whether [we be] Jews or Gentiles, whether [we be] bond or free; and have been all made to drink into one Spirit. For the body is not one member, but many.

"If the foot shall say, Because I am not the hand, I am not of the body; is it therefore not of the body? And if the ear shall say, Because I am not the eye, I am not of the body; is it therefore not of the body? If the whole body [were] an eye, where [were] the hearing? If the whole [were] hearing, where [were] the smelling?

"But now hath God set the members every one of them in the body, as it hath pleased him. And if they were all one member, where [were] the body? But now [are they] many members, yet but one body. And the eye cannot say unto the hand, I have no need of thee: nor again the head to the feet, I have no need of you. Nay, much more those members of the body, which seem to be more feeble, are necessary:

"And those [members] of the body, which we think to be less honorable, upon these we bestow more abundant honour; and our uncomely [parts] have more abundant comeliness. For our comely [parts] have no need: but God hath tempered the body together, having given more abundant honour to that [part] which lacked: That there should be no schism in the body; but [that] the members should have the same care one for another. And whether one member suffer, all the members suffer with it; or one member be honoured, all the members rejoice with it. Now ye are the body of Christ, and members in particular."

All members of the body of Christ have been given at least one gift of the spirit. Each member has an obligation to identify and use their gift(s) for the benefit of the whole. If members withhold their gifts, they handicap the church of Christ and makes it incomplete. The members rely on each others' strengths and gifts to obtain their unifying purpose of eternal life. Hence, the counsel: "Let every man stand in his own office, and labor in his own calling; and let not the head say unto the feet it hath no need of the feet; for without the feet how shall the body be able to stand? Also the body hath need of every member, that all may be edified together, that the system may be kept perfect."[10]

It is possible to gain unity in diversity. We gain unity through being united in Christ and being one in the purpose of gaining happiness and eternal life. We experience diversity from the fact that each individual is unique and makes a contribution according to his specific talents, gifts, and abilities to the cause of helping all gain happiness and eternal life.

Story on Diversity

"The Animal School" by Dr. R. H. Reeves

Once upon a time, the animals decided they must do something heroic to meet the problems of a "New World," so they organized a school. They adopted an activity curriculum consisting of running, climbing, swimming and flying. To make it easier to administer, all animals took all the subjects.

The duck was excellent in swimming, better in fact than his instructor, and made excellent grades in flying, but he was very poor in running. Since he was low in running he had to stay after school and also drop swimming to practice running. This was kept up until his web feet were badly worn and he was only average in swimming, but average was acceptable in school, so nobody worried about that except the duck.

The rabbit started at the top of the class in running, but had a nervous breakdown because of so much makeup in swimming.

The squirrel was excellent in climbing until he developed frustration in flying class where his teacher made him start from the ground up instead of from the tree-top down. He also developed charley horses from over-exertion and he got a C in climbing and a D in running.

The eagle was a problem child and had to be disciplined severely. In climbing class, he beat all the others to the top of the tree, but insisted on using his own way of getting there.

At the end of the year, an abnormal eel that could swim exceedingly well and also could run, climb and fly a little had the highest average and was valedictorian.

The prairie dogs stayed out of school and fought the tax levy because the administration would not add digging and burrowing to the curriculum. They apprenticed their children to the badger and later joined the groundhogs and gophers to start a successful private school.

Relationships

"I don't think of leadership as a position.
I don't think of leadership as a skill.
I think of leadership as a relationship."
—Phil Quigley, Pacific Bell

Humans are social. With very few exceptions, we seek friends and community. We desire friends; we wish for love; we value the opinions and esteem of others. In many cases, we determine our own self-value through feed-back from the people around us. By the same token, loneliness is often the greatest tragedy of a person's life. Films and literature discuss the terrible pain of those of who are unloved, abused, and rejected.

In a generic sense, the word relationship simply implies that two separate bodies interact with each other, that they are connected. As soon as two people recognize each other's existence they have a relationship in a general way. A relationship as such has, most likely, very little significance. The significance of relationships usually grows as we become familiar and intimate with people. Most of us find ourselves in many different relationships of varying levels of intimacy.

For some reason, we need other people to interact positively with us. We need a relationship with them that differs from our relationship with anything else in the universe (with, perhaps, the exception of God). For the vast majority of humanity, neither plants, animals, nor inanimate objects fulfill this need. Most of our fundamental human needs are fulfilled with relationships with people. The need to be accepted, understood, respected, valued, to feel important and secure, and to contribute to a purpose higher than self are fulfilled through relationships with people.

Why do we need others? Why are we social? Why are other people so important to us? The answers to these questions may never be given adequately by philosophy or psychology or even, perhaps, religion. In fact, Christ basically assumed this need, and took the next step of suggesting that we make other people the center of our lives by loving and serving them. Our relationships with one another are so significant to the Lord that He has told us that the way we will be recognized as his disciples is by the way we treat one another and the priority we place on each other. "By this shall all men know that ye are my disciples, if ye have love one to another" (John 13:35). Thus, as leaders, it is our challenge to cultivate and value relationships like the Savior.

One challenge of a leader is finding a balance between ministering (serving) and administering (organizing, planning, etc.) So many times in organizations production seems to be the major focus and the people and their development get left somewhere in the background. Divine-Centered Leaders put people first. They put people before programs, schedules, and production. Christ dedicated his whole life to loving and serving people. Christ didn't spend a lot of time in an office by himself. He spent his time with people. Should our lives be any different?

Relationships are fundamental to leadership because an effective relationship must exist for one person to influence another. The keys to effective relationships are the same as those of effective leadership. All of the concepts discussed in this book (unity, agency, excellence, managing conflict, integrity, leading by the spirit, diversity, etc.) help to cultivate better relationships. But above all these concepts, there is one foundational principle that is the key to relationships—love.

12 Principles for Cultivating Loving Relationships

"Individuals grow but teams explode."
—Lennon Ledbetter

1. Don't Criticize.

Follow this simple rule: If you don't have anything nice to say, don't say anything at all. Make this a rule you live by. Do not give in to the temptation to say negative things about people even if they are true. There is a tendency for people to say negative comments about those around them and to gossip about the faults of others—don't be a part of it. If you say negative things about individuals not present, you are sending a message to those who are present that you would do the same to them. The way to gain the respect and loyalty of those present is to be respectful and loyal to those who are not present.

If constructive criticism (feedback) is necessary for a specific person, it should be done in private with love and the intent of helping them. Don't correct them in front of others. Also, talk about what they do well, what you like about them, and your own mistakes before correcting theirs.

2. Give Sincere Compliments

People need and want to be complimented. Compliments bring out the best efforts in people. If you desire to uplift or motivate someone, a powerful way to do it is by complimenting them. Always look for opportunities to compliment those around you. Even if people make mistakes, focus on their successful efforts, and compliment them on those items. The natural tendency is to tell people what they did wrong and get mad at them. This will result in a decrease of motivation and performance.

I (Cameron) remember a time when I was running the hurdles in high school and was greatly motivated by compliments. I was plagued with several injuries, was in great pain, and had difficulty practicing and competing. Doctors told me there was no way I could compete and that I was putting myself at risk for more serious injuries. There were times when it was hard to walk, and I needed help getting in and out of the car. I was considering quitting track. While I was debating quitting, another hurdler (Steve Talbot, the best hurdler in the state at the time) that I was working out with made this comment, "You have the best hurdling form I have ever seen. I think you have the ability to win state." It was this compliment and his continuing encouragement and compliments that kept me from quitting and brought out my best performance. That year I ended up doing extremely well and became one of the all-time best hurdlers in our high school's history. If I would have received negative comments and criticism or simple no compliments, I may have quit. Encouragement is a much more effective teaching device than criticism.

3. Smile, and Be Happy

"Happiness is a decision you make."
—Lennon Ledbetter

Actions speak louder than words, and a smile says, "I like you. You make me happy. I'm glad to see you." People who smile tend to manage and teach more effectively. Another principle is this: "Choose to be Happy." We have the ability to choose how we respond to negative stimulus such as bad weather, people yelling or saying bad things about us, not accomplishing purposes, etc. None of these stimuli can make us sad, angry, or frustrated unless we choose to respond in such a way. Choose now to be happy no matter what the circumstances, and you will always be happy. Happiness doesn't depend on outward conditions but on those inside.

4. Remember Peoples Name

Remembering a person's name and using it easily is a subtle and very effective compliment. But forget it or misspell it and you have placed yourself at a sharp disadvantage. Take the time and effort to memorize each person's name whom you associate with. When someone tells you their name, make sure you heard it correctly. Then memorize it by repeating it in your mind, associating it with something, and when possible, write it down.[12]

5. If Offended, Take the Initiative

"Why is the initiative with the one who has been offended, when the natural tendency when we are offended is to say within ourselves, 'He is the one at fault; therefore, he should come to me.' Oftentimes a person offends unknowingly. If someone offends you knowingly and continues to do so, you are responsible for the strain in the relationship if you do not take the initiative to clear it up. Often you'll find you made unrealistic expectations. You may discover you simply didn't understand the situation at all...

Consider two tragic consequences of not taking the initiative. First, the one offended often broods about the offense until the situation is blown all out of proportion. Like a poison, bitterness and resentment spread and afflict other relationships and situations totally removed from the initial one. Then guilt grows within causing anger to flash and bite; feeding on the weaknesses of others. Eventually the mounting vindictive spirit can contain itself no longer, and it explodes irrationally at the slightest provocation on its 'enemy' inflicting wounds and scars that may never be healed. Now the whole problem has changed both in location and in complexity. The offended becomes the offender.

Second, sometimes we have expectations of another, and when he doesn't come through, we are offended. We then judge and behave defensively to avoid further hurt. The other sees this defensiveness and may react similarly, thus giving us new evidence to support our earlier judgments. We, the offended, bring about the very treatment we feared. This is the self-fulfilling prophecy.[13]

6. Return Good for Evil

"Hatred is never ended with hatred but by love."
—Buddha

We have a natural tendency to treat others as they treat us. If someone is mean to us, we are mean back. If someone is nice to us, we are nice back. If someone hates us, we hate them. If someone shows us love, we love them. If someone helps us, we want to help them. The Savior teaches us to not respond in the natural way of returning good for good and evil for evil but to always respond with goodness. The Savior emphasizes the need to return good for evil in Matthew 5:38- 40,43,44, "Ye have heard that it hath been said, An eye for an eye, and a tooth for a tooth: But I say unto you, That ye resist not evil: but whosoever shall smite thee on thy right cheek, turn to him the other also. And if a man sue thee at the law, and take away thy coat, let him have thy cloke also. Ye have heard that it hath been said, Thou shalt love thy neighbour, and hate thine enemy. But I say unto you, Love your enemies, bless them that curse you, do good to them that hate you, and pray for them which despitefully use you, and persecute you."

The natural tendency to respond in the same manner which others treat us is called the law of reciprocity. The law of reciprocity results in either better or worse relationships. For example, if someone is mean to you, you respond naturally and are mean back. Since you are mean to them they are mean again, so you also respond again with meanness. This produces a cyclical effect with each person returning more and more meanness creating a destructive relationship.

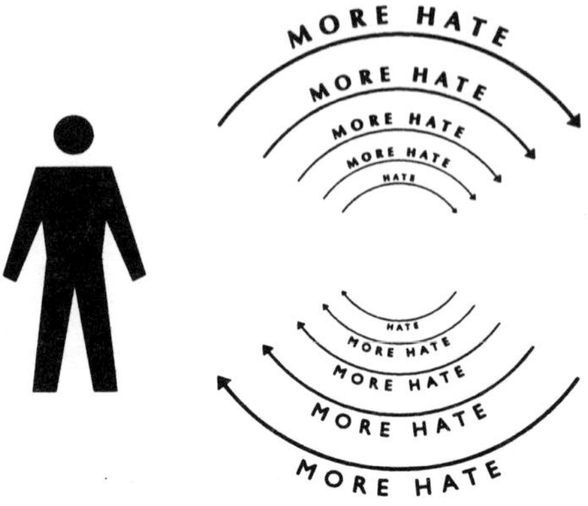

Negative Reciprocity Cycle

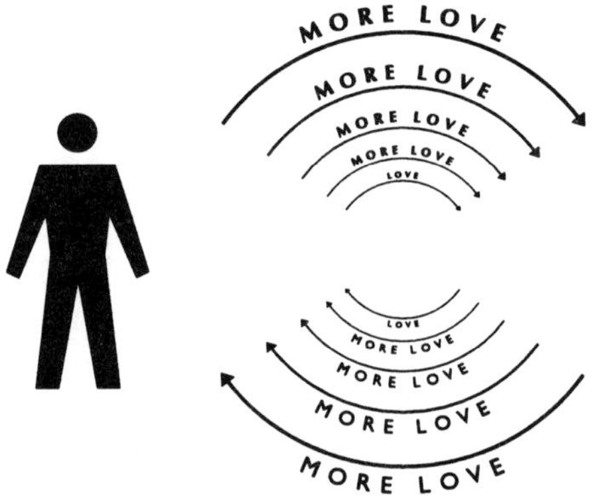

Positive Reciprocity Cycle

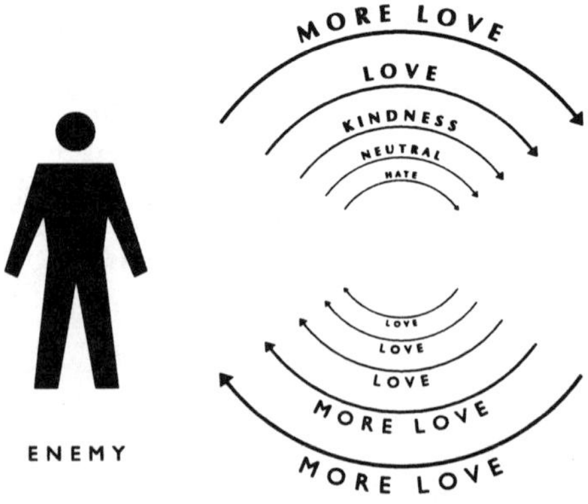

Reversing the Reciprocity Cycle

The law of reciprocity can also work in the positive direction. For example, if you show someone kindness and love, they will respond naturally with kindness which makes you want to respond with even more kindness and love. This produces a cyclical effect where each returns more and more kindness and love to produce a more and more loving relationship.

The Lord's command to return love for hate, concern and prayer for persecution, blessing for cursing enables us to turn the negative cycle in the law of reciprocity to a positive one. Reversing the reciprocity cycle can result in turning enemies into friends. For example, your enemy says unkind things to you and you respond by complimenting him on his good qualities. Your enemy damages your property so you respond by taking him cookies. As you continue to return good acts, your enemy will have no desire to perform evil acts and will instead have a desire to respond with good actions. As your enemy ceases to perform negative acts and performs positive ones, the reciprocity cycle has been reversed and you begin building a friendship with a former enemy.

7. Keep Commitments

Keeping commitments is vital to having a successful relationship. There's probably nothing more destructive than to make a promise that's important to someone and then not come through. The next time a promise is made, they won't believe it. Breaking commitments destroys trust within a relationship.

Divine-Centered Leaders adopt a philosophy never to make a promise they can't or won't keep. They make promises very carefully and sparingly and are aware of as many variables as possible so that something doesn't suddenly keep them from fulfilling the promise.

Occasionally, despite all our best efforts, the unexpected does come up, creating a situation where it would be unwise or impossible to keep a promise. But Divine-Centered Leaders value the promise and either keep the promise anyway or explain the situation thoroughly to the person involved and ask to be released from the promise. As we keep promises, we build trust and reliability within our relationships.[14]

8. Follow the Golden Rule

The Savior sums up well how to cultivate loving relationships with the golden rule, "Whatsoever ye would that men should do to you, do ye even so to them."[15]

9. Sacrifice for the Person

"Sacrifice is a demonstration of love. When we are willing to forego something we have, want or could have for another person's benefit, we increase in love for that person. Parents' love for children grows continually because of sacrifices of time, money, health, sometimes food and clothing, luxuries, etc. for the children. Children who would increase in love for their parents sacrifice for their parents throughout the growing years as well as when parents become less able to care for themselves. Anyone can sacrifice for another person, if they want to and will. Friends can sacrifice for friends. Teachers can sacrifice for students. Employees can sacrifice for employers. Results will be an increase of love on the part of the one doing the sacrificing."[16]

10. Take Time to be with the Person and Do things Together

"Perhaps time is the greatest thing we have to give someone we love or would love. We have to give opportunity for love to increase and for expressions of that love. Isn't it strange that so many expressions of genuine love come following time together when an activity, event, experience, joy, sorrow, struggle, or challenge was shared. As we demonstrate our willingness to make time available for another, we say to them 'I am willing to give you the most precious thing I have—my time. I do this because I love you and you are important to me.'"[17]

11. Accept the Person as He is

"We will never love a person until we can accept the individual as he is. This doesn't mean we agree with nor accept the person's behavior, nor does it mean that we won't want the individual to change. It does mean we are willing without reservation to accept the person as an important human being. We want to be with the person. We want the person to be with us. We avoid letting little things the person does bother us. As we increase in ability to accept the person as he is and genuinely communicate that acceptance to him, we will increase in love for that person."[18]

12. Tell the Individual, "I Love You!"

"When we genuinely communicate verbally to another person, "I love you!" there is an emotional reaction heart to heart which causes each to realize that love exists. The act is complete when the person responds genuinely back, "I love you too." Even when the other person does not respond back to our statement of love, we increase in our ability to love through verbal expression."[19]

Story on Relationships

"It was a Good Barn" by Edward Ziegler

An old friendship had grown cold. Where once there had been closeness, there was only strain. Now pride kept me from picking up the phone.

Then one day I dropped in on another old friend, who's had a long career as a minister and counselor. We were seated in his study—surrounded by maybe a thousand books—and fell into deep conversation about everything from small computers to the tormented life of Beethoven.

The subject finally turned to friendship and how perishable it seems to be these days. I mentioned my own experience as an example. "Relationships are mysteries," my friend said.

"Some endure. Others fall apart."

Gazing out his window to the wooded Vermont hills, he pointed toward a neighboring farm and said, "There used to be a large barn over there." Next to a red-frame house were the footings of what had been a sizable structure.

He continued, "It was solidly built, probably in the 1870s. But like so many of the places around here, it went down because people left for richer lands in the Midwest. No one took care of the barn. Its roof needed patching; rainwater got under the eaves and dripped down inside the posts and beams.

One day a high wind came along, and the whole barn began to tremble. You could hear this creaking, first, like old sailing-ship timbers, and then a sharp series of cracks and a tremendous roaring sound. Suddenly it was a heap of scrap lumber.

After the storm blew over, I went down and saw these beautiful, old oak timbers, solid as could be. I asked the fellow who owns the place what had happened. He said he figured the rainwater had settled in the pinholes, where wooden dowels held the joints together. Once those pins were rotted, there was nothing to link the giant beams together."

We both gazed down the hill. Now all that was left of the barn was its cellar hole and its border of lilac shrubs.

My friend said he had turned the incident over and over in is mind, and finally came to recognize some parallels between building a barn and building a friendship: no matter how strong you are, how notable your attainments, you have enduring significance only in your relationship to others.

"To make your life a sound structure that will serve others and fulfill your own potential," he said, "you have to remember that strength, however massive, can't endure unless it has the interlocking support of others. Go it alone and you'll inevitably tumble."

"Relationships have to be cared for," he added, "like the roof of a barn. Letters unwritten, thanks unsaid, confidences violated, quarrels unsettled—all these act like rainwater seeping into the pegs, weakening the link between the beams."

My friend shook his head. "It was a good barn. And it would have taken very little to keep it in good repair. Now it will probably never be rebuilt."

Later that afternoon I got ready to leave. "You wouldn't like to borrow my phone to make a call, I don't suppose?" he asked.

"Yes," I said, "I think I would. Very much."

Application Ideas for Cultivating Loving Relationships

12 Principles for Cultivating Loving Relationships

1. Don't Criticize
2. Give Sincere Compliments
3. Smile, and Be Happy
4. Remember People's Name, and Call them by Name
5. If Offended, Take the Initiative
6. Return Good for Evil
7. Keep Commitments
8. Follow the Golden Rule
9. Sacrifice for the Person
10. Take Time to be with the Person and Do Things Together
11. Accept the Person as He is
12. Tell the Individual, "I Love You!"

1. Review the 12 principles for cultivating loving relationships and identify those that you may violate in your relationships. Set goals to adjust your behavior in these relationships to be in harmony with the 12 principles.

2. Choose one or two relationships that you would like to improve. Set a goal to apply some of the 12 principles for cultivating a loving relationship during the coming week.

Communication

Communication is one of the most important skills in life. Almost everything we do involves communication. We must communicate effectively in order to Show the Way.

Communication occurs between people. To communicate effectively we must understand the needs of people. Maslow's hierarchy of needs shows how understanding the needs of others can help us to communicate more effectively.

The hierarchic theory can be represented as a pyramid, with the larger, lower levels representing the lower needs, and the upper point representing the need for self-actualization. Maslow's hierarchic theory of human needs gives the order in which we satisfy our needs. The base of the pyramid is physiological needs—the need for food, water, warmth, oxygen, etc. The next level is security needs—the need to feel safe from present or future harm and threat. The next level is social needs—the need to feel accepted, understood , and respected by others. The next level is ego needs—the need for self-worth, self-respect, to be someone of importance. The next level is the need for self-actualization or self-fulfillment—the need to be creative, to contribute, to grow.

Maslow's theory of needs has affected many fields of study, including communication. How does it apply to communication? One of the fundamental ideas of Maslow is that there is a specific order in which we fulfill our needs. Fulfilling needs is sequential and we seek to fulfill basic needs first. We must fulfill our physiological needs before we seek to fulfill our security needs, social or ego needs. For example, what would happen if right now all the air was taken

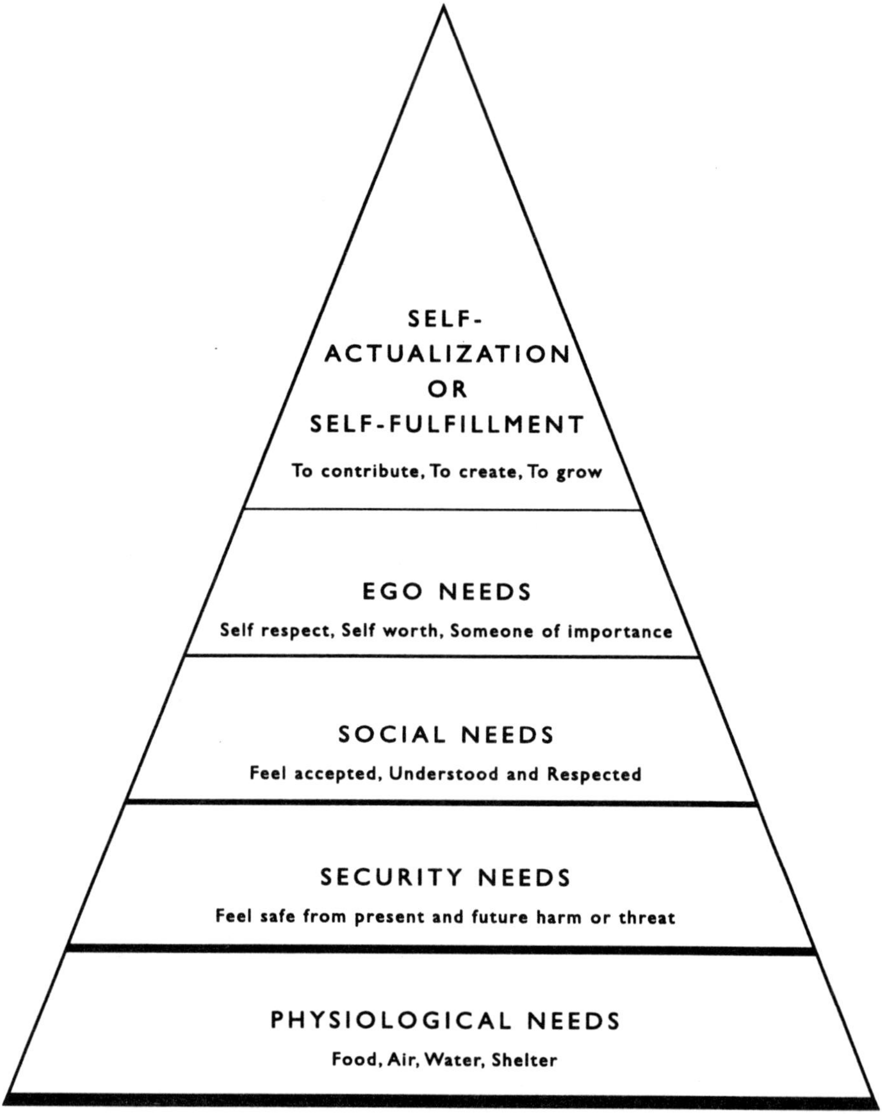

Maslow's Hierarchy of Needs

out of the room you are now in? What would happen to your interest in this book? Your only desire would be to fulfill your need for air. Could I get you to read the book by making it more interesting, adding more pictures, paying you to read it, or helping you understand its importance? No. Air is a fundamental physical need, and until that need is met, you will not be interested in anything else. However, once you have fulfilled your need for air, your interest can shift to other things. Then my tactics may have some effect in influencing you to read the book. Once we fulfill our physiological needs, we seek to fulfill our security needs. And once our security needs are fulfilled, we seek to fulfill our social needs, etc. There is an order and process in which we seek to fulfill our needs. This hierarchical order greatly affects how we need to communicate.

Applying the Hierarchy of Needs to Communication

We will assume that the physiological needs—need for food, water, air, etc.—are satisfied. The next level of needs is the need for security—the need to feel safe from present or future harm and threat. In order for communication to occur, there must be a sense of trust between individuals; a feeling that the other person will not harm them and that communication will not result in harm or damage. If we seek to communicate before the need for security is fulfilled, the communication will be superficial and ineffective. The need for security in communication is fulfilled through our relationship with them.

Communication takes place within relationships, so the effectiveness of our communication depends on the nature and quality of our relationships. There must be an element of love and trust. Love is vital to communication because it creates an environment of trust where each individual can communicate openly, honestly, and directly. It creates an atmosphere of safety and trust. Communicating can make one vulnerable and people are not willing to make themselves vulnerable unless there is an element of love that guards against hurt or ridicule. The need for security must be fulfilled for communication to take place.

The next level of needs are social—the need to feel accepted, understood, and respected by others. We fulfill social needs by having others understand us. When other people understand us, we feel accepted and somehow connected to them because they understand us—fulfilling our need to be accepted and understood. When someone else understands us, even though they may disagree, the fact that they understood us tells us they respect our opinion enough to learn it.

The next level of needs are ego—the need to be someone of importance, a person of significance. These needs are not fulfilled simply by being understood—they are fulfilled when someone wants to understand us and seeks to understand us. When someone seeks to understand us they are saying, "You are important," "I care about you," "You are worth listening to, a person of significance, a person that matters."

The hierarchal needs are the same for everyone and this can cause problems in communication. We all desire to be understood and it is our natural tendency to seek first to be understood by others before we seek to understand them. We seek to fulfill our needs first. As two people discuss an idea or problem, they both want to be understood and aren't interested in the view of the other person until their view is understood. So the two fight to be understood, not seeking to understand the other. Thus neither feels understood because neither person is listening and neither of their needs to be understood are met. This can result in arguing and fighting; sometimes the raising of voices in hopes that by shouting the other person might understand what we are saying. We try to force the other person to understand us and that doesn't work.

For example, how often do parents try to get their children to do something or tell them something and the child responds, "You don't understand what I am going through," "You don't know how I feel." "You don't know what it is like." The child will not listen to anything the parents are telling them. The child is saying, "I need to be understood." The parents also want to be understood so they try harder to convey their message; wondering why the child won't listen. The child won't listen because the need to be understood has not been met and, until that need is fulfilled, they can't focus their attention elsewhere. The child will not accept advice or counsel from the parents until their need to be understood is met.

First Listen to Understand, Then Speak to Be Understood

If we understand that people need to be understood before they can seek to understand, we will approach communication with the correct attitude. As we first listen to understand, then speak to be understood, we will have a much different experience than when both people seek to be understood. As we understand the person we are communicating with, we fulfill the social and ego needs of the individual thus enabling them to understand another's view or ideas. This creates a discussion where both are understood by the other resulting in mutual respect and acceptance.

Communication involves two processes: the process of conveying a message so that we are clearly understood and the process of receiving a message with its intended meaning. We have a natural desire to seek first to be understood and then to understand. When both people have this attitude, contention and trying to force understanding will result. When both people are seeking to be understood, it is like trying to force a person to read a book when there is no air in the room. It just doesn't work. A wise person will approach communication with the attitude of first listening to understand, then speaking to be understood.

How do we understand each other? By listening. There are generally considered to be five different levels of listening.

1. Ignoring the other person.
2. Pretending to listen.
3. Selective listening—where we hear only those things we want to hear.
4. Attentive listening—where we focus on the words and phrases used but do not try to reach the speaker's level of feeling.
5. Listening to Understand—listening with the intent to understand the other person's frame of reference.

So we truly understand others not by listening only but by listening to understand. How do we listen to understand?

1. Listening from the others person's frame of reference.
2. Seeking to understand not only what they say, but also how they feel.
3. Listening with our ears and our heart.

Listening to understand is characterized by:

1. Asking questions so that the sender feels free to tell you more.
2. Repeating what the sender has said so he will know you are listening.
3. Being calm and alert.
4. Maintaining eye contact.

Poor listening is characterized by:

1. Frequently interrupting.
2. Premature advice.
3. Making irrelevant comments.
4. Giving a blank look.

We can know that we understand another's communication by restating what we understood the person to say and then allowing him to tell us whether we understood correctly. Do not assume that you understand what the person is trying to say and what they are feeling. Misunderstandings occur all the time; even at times when we think we understood them clearly. Restating what we think the others person is saying and feeling and allowing them to clarify can alleviate misunderstandings. As said Gandhi, "Three-fourths of the miseries and misunderstandings in the world will disappear if we step into the shoes of our adversaries and understand their standpoint."[20]

We have discussed how we understand others through listening to understand. We must also be able to communicate in a way that others understand us. The process of first listening to understand, and then speaking to be understood also plays a vital role in effectively conveying our thoughts and feelings. Our feelings and thoughts are based upon how we perceive situations so we need to make sure we correctly understand the situation before we act. Oftentimes when we come to understand the situation, how we feel and what we think are greatly changed. As our understanding of the situation changes so does the message we desire to communicate.

The following story of a miscommunication between an English lady and a school master helps to illustrate this point. It seems that a little old English lady was looking for some rooms in Switzerland. She asked the local village school master to help her. A place that suited her was finally found and the lady returned to London for her luggage. She remembered then that she had not noticed a bathroom, or as she called it, a "water closet." So she wrote to the school master. He was puzzled by the initials "W.C.," never dreaming, of course, that she was asking about a bathroom. He finally asked the help of the parish priest who decided that W.C. stood for Wesleyan Church. This was his reply:

Dear Madam,

The W.C. is situated nine miles from the house in the center of a beautiful grove of trees. It is capable of holding 350 people at a time and is open on Tuesday, Thursday and Sunday each week. A large number of folks attend during the summer months, so it is suggested you go early, although there is plenty of standing room. Some folks like to take their lunch and make a day of it, especially on Thursday when there is organ accompaniment. The acoustics are very good and everyone can hear the slightest sound.

It may be of interest to you to know that my daughter was married in our W.C. and it was there she met her husband.

We hope you will be there in time for our bazaar to be held very soon. The proceeds will go towards the purchase of plush seats which the folks agree are a long-felt need, as the present seats all have holes in them.

My wife is rather delicate, therefore she cannot attend regularly. It has been six months since the last time she went. Naturally, it pains her very much not to be able to go more often.

I shall close now with the desire to accommodate you in every way possible and I will be happy to save you a seat down front or near the door, which ever you prefer.

School Master

In the above example, the School Master assumed that he understood the situation. If he would have sought first to understand, his perception of the situation would have been greatly changed and the message he would have conveyed would have been extremely different. When our understanding of a situation changes, so does our thoughts, behavior, feelings, and communication.

So not only does first listening to understand, then speaking to be understood facilitate communication by fulfilling others' social and ego needs, it also results in the improvement of messages we convey because we better understand the situation and circumstances we are responding to.

How do we communicate so that others understand us, our perceptions and our feelings? To effectively communicate our feelings with others, we need to be honest, open, and direct. There are many situations where we conceal our feelings or are not completely honest with others. Why? The main reason we hesitate to be honest and open is because of fear. We are afraid of the response, afraid of how the other person may feel, afraid to cause conflict or afraid of confrontation. Because of fear, it takes courage to communicate our feelings and thoughts.

Honesty is the best policy in communication. We should let others know how we feel even though it is hard and even if it may initially cause pain because in the long run it will be for the best. Of course, there are times when it is not best to be open, honest, and direct in communicating but these times are the exception not the rule. I can tell you that being honest and open is the best way to communicate, but you will never know for sure until you try it yourself. Don't let fear compel you to be closed and dishonest in relationships.

Application Ideas for Communicating Effectively

1. In your communication with others, first listen to understand, then speak to be understood. For example, if someone is late, don't immediately respond by getting upset, but first try to understand why they are late and then respond.

2. Identify relationships in which you are not completely honest, open and direct; such as in a dating relationship or with a friend who does things that bother you but you never express how their actions make you feel. Set a goal to be more honest in these relationships and take the courage to be open, honest, and direct. If there is an element of love and trust in the relationship being honest, open, and direct will better it.

3. The key to having honest and open communication in a relationship is establishing that as the method of communication. Have each person commit to being honest, open and direct and to expect that from the other person. As we let others know we want them to be honest and open with us, they will be more willing to express their feelings. Let them know that you want them to be honest and open with you even if what they have to say may not be what you want to hear. Asking people to be honest and open helps reduce the fear of communicating our ideas and feelings because we know the other person is expecting and desiring it.

4. An effective way to communicate displeasure with someone is through I-messages. Mutual trust is destroyed when we blame others for our feelings or condemn others for their behavior. "You" messages tend to be critical, condemning the person instead of their behavior. For example, "You bother me." However, using I-messages, we are able to tell others how we feel about their behavior without judging them.

An I-message usually consists of three parts:

1. Reference to the person's behavior
2. How the I-message sender feels about it
3. Why the I-message sender feels that way

For example, " (1)When you don't take your turn washing the dishes, (2) I feel angry (3) because our house gets messy and then I have to do your work.

I-messages may not always change other people's behavior, but they do let others know how you feel without condemning them and this opens the way to problem resolution. Listening to understand lets others know that you understand how they feel and I-messages helps others understand how you feel.

Servant Leadership

"Within the kingdom of God, to lead is to serve."
—Spencer J. Condie

"The servant-leader is servant first. It begins with the natural feeling that one wants to serve, to serve first. Then conscious choice brings one to aspire to lead. That person is sharply different from one who is a leader first, perhaps because of the need to assuage an unusual power drive or to acquire material possessions. For such it will be a later choice to serve—after leadership is established. The leader-first and the servant-first are two extreme types. Between them there are shadings and blends that are part of the infinite variety of human nature. The difference manifests itself in the care taken by the servant-first to make sure that other people's highest priority needs are being served. The best test, and difficult to administer, is: Do those served grow as persons? Do they, while being served, become healthier, wiser, freer, more autonomous, more likely them-selves to become servants?"[21]

Divine-Centered Leaders are servants first while many world leaders are leaders first to their followers. Jesus teaches the importance of being a servant to those we lead and not to lead as the world does in Matthew 20:25-28, "Ye know that the princes of the Gentiles exercise dominion over them, and they that are great exercise authority upon them. But it shall not be so among you: but whosoever will be great among you, let him be your minister; And whosoever will be chief among you, let him be your servant: Even as the Son of man came not to be ministered unto, but to minister."

Divine-Centered Leaders are servants to those they lead. As leaders we have a responsibility to fulfill our follower's needs and help them learn and grow and become servant-leaders also.

Application Idea for Servant Leadership

1. Identify your various leadership roles, and various stewardships. Ask yourself the following questions to identify if your leadership is in line with the Master's method of servant leadership. "Do I ask my followers to do things that will benefit me or things that will benefit them," and "Am I motived to action because I want to fulfill my needs and responsibilities or because I want to fulfill the needs of others?"

Stewardship

"He that is a faithful and wise steward shall inherit all things."

Leadership, in its very essence, is a stewardship in which an individual is given responsibility over someone or something. Also, by giving our followers stewardships, we help them learn and grow. This being the case, it is vital for us to understand the stewardship principles and how we can become and help others become "wise and faithful stewards."[22]

Christ gave us considerable insight into the principle of stewardship in the parable of the talents found in Matthew 25:14-30:

"For [the kingdom of heaven is] as a man travelling into a far country, [who] called his own servants, and delivered unto them his goods. And unto one he gave five talents, to another two, and to another one; to every man according to his several ability; and straightway took his journey. Then he that had received the five talents went and traded with the same, and made [them] other five talents. And likewise he that [had received] two, he also gained other two. But he that had received one went and digged in the earth, and hid his lord's money.

"After a long time the lord of those servants cometh, and reckoneth with them. And so he that had received five talents came and brought other five talents, saying, Lord, thou deliveredst unto me five talents: behold, I have gained beside them five talents more.

His lord said unto him, Well done, [thou] good and faithful servant: thou hast been faithful over a few things, I will make thee ruler over many things: enter thou into the joy of thy lord. He also that had received two talents came and said, Lord, thou deliveredst unto me two talents: behold, I have gained two other talents beside them. His lord said unto him, Well done, good and faithful servant; thou hast been faithful over a few things, I will make thee ruler over many things: enter thou into the joy of thy lord.

"Then he which had received the one talent came and said, Lord, I knew thee that thou art an hard man, reaping where thou hast not sown, and gathering where thou hast not strawed: And I was afraid, and went and hid thy talent in the earth: lo, [there] thou hast [that is] thine. His lord answered and said unto him, [Thou] wicked and slothful servant, thou knewest that I reap where I sowed not, and gather where I have not strawed: Thou oughtest therefore to have put my money to the exchangers, and [then] at my coming I should have received mine own with usury. Take therefore the talent from him, and give [it] unto him which hath ten talents. For unto every one that hath shall be given, and he shall have abundance: but from him that hath not shall be taken away even that which he hath. And cast ye the unprofitable servant into outer darkness: there shall be weeping and gnashing of teeth."

To begin with, we learn from this parable that stewardship involves entrusting something that is yours into the hands of another (v.14). The Lord frequently gives His children stewardship opportunities. He gives parents the responsibility of raising His children. He asks us to watch over and care for one anothers. The list continues. Giving a stewardship to another involves risk, because there is always the possibility that the stewardship will be neglected. However, it is important to delegate stewardships so that individuals can learn and grow.

A second lesson from this parable is that once we have assigned a stewardship, we must give them the opportunity to magnify it. In this parable, the master leaves for a time. Likewise, we must give people the time, space and trust they need to magnify their assigned stewardship.

Another lesson learned is that a large part of stewardship is accountability. When the master returns, he asks his servants to account for their assigned stewardships (v.19). The Lord teaches us the principle of accountability time and time again in the scriptures. "It is required of the Lord, at the hand of every steward, to render an account of his stewardship, both in time and in eternity. For he who is faithful and wise in time is accounted worthy to inherit the mansions prepared for him of my Father."[23] Marion G. Romney has made the wise comment that "if we as leaders want the support of those we lead, then we will do well to share with them a report on how our assigned stewardship is doing."[24] Thus, accountability and reporting apply to both leader and follower. We must be accountable to one another in our assigned stewardships.

We also learn from this parable that we should assign stewardships according to individual capacity (v.15). In Spencer W. Kimball's article "Jesus: the Perfect Leader," he makes the following statement: "Jesus gave people truths and tasks that were matched to their capacity. He did not overwhelm them with more than they could manage, but gave them enough to stretch their souls." The master in this parable knew that one of his servants could handle five talents while another could be stretched with only one.

In addition to these lessons, we also learn from the parable what the role of a steward is. Stewards are not merely assigned to watch over and maintain something. Part of stewardship is improving what you were initially given. J. Richard Clark has said, "To be profitable servants, we must improve that which the Lord has entrusted to us. Stewards are managers, and sound management reduces waste and ensures an appropriate return on invested resources."[25] The requirement of improving what you were given is clearly seen in the parable of the talents. The "good and faithful" servants were those who improved on what they had been given. However, the servant who hid his talent was seen by the master as an unprofitable servant and was cast into outer darkness.

Continuum of Leadership Styles

AUTOCRATIC--------------PERSUADING--------------DEMOCRATIC--------------DELEGATING
RULE CENTERED--PRINCIPLE CENTERED
TRAINING WHEELS--21-SPEED MOUNTAIN BIKE

Authority: 100% Leader, 0% Group	Authority: 75% Leader, 25% Group	Authority: 49% Leader, 51% Group	Authority: 25% Leader, 75% Group
Gives orders and tells subordinates what they are to do and when and how they are to do it.	Persuades the group to follow the leader.	Believes in sharing information, authority, responsibility, and accountability.	Provide vision, direction, and purpose but allows follower to determine how to obtain.
Compels subordinates to perform at his command, and is quick to remind them if they don't.	Sells way of thinking and ideas to the group.	Everyone concerned is involved in the decision-making and implementation process.	Turns problems over to individuals or goups.
Is the authority; His way is the only way.	Makes decisions and expects subordinates to endorse and follow them.	Sees strength in being open and discussing ideas.	Willing to accept decisions of goup within the established limits.
Obeys superiors as he expects to be obeyed by those he leads.	Wants followers fully informed.	Believes that if people are informed they will make decisions that are best for themselves.	Tries to build cooperation and team spirit.
Tells subordinates only what they need to know to get the job done.	Used when subordinates feel inferior to the leader.	Oraganization needed to complete a task that will often develop spontaneously.	Wants group members to have mutual respect for each other.
Selects loyal assistants.	Tries to understand the thinking and actions of his followers.	Leader sets goals with those who he leads.	More effective with cooperative individuals.
Makes it clear that obedience to instructions is essential to success.	Requires effort to teach and communicate ideas.	Role is more as a coodinator.	Each person has a role in the total job to be done.
		More concerned with the group than with himself.	

Leadership Styles

"To the man who only has a hammer, everything he encounters begins to look like a nail."
—Abraham Maslow

There are many principles of effective leadership that apply to all people. However, each individual is different and the abilities of our followers will vary. Thus, we must vary our leadership styles to that which will be most effective in helping individuals learn and grow.

Leaders must find the right leadership style for their followers. When the style of leadership doesn't match the style of followership in a group, conflict almost certainly ensues. A leader may feel that he gets no respect; a follower may feel condescended to, or left in a lurch. Often, using the wrong style can mean an immediate end to a leader's credibility within a group.

Good leaders must be flexible. We all have a preferred leadership style, but we must learn to adapt our styles to the group. Some of us may need to "get tough," and become a little more dictatorial. Others must learn to "let go of the reins," and allow people more freedom.

Perhaps the first thing we notice when working with a leader is his or her style. Almost immediately we sense how much he wishes to control or be involved in our work. In some cases, we cringe at the oppressive style of a leader; other times, we would do anything if the leader would just tell us what he wants.

These two examples represent extremes in leadership styles. All leaders have a comfortable style, and perhaps a "backup" they use when their normal style doesn't work. A leader's style falls along a continuum (see figure p. 139) which ranges from a very autocratic, dictatorial style (on the left) to a delegating style (on the right). The amount of authority the leader exercises decreases as the continuum moves from left to right while the freedom of the group increases.

Is one leadership style more effective than another? No. It is not where the style lies on the continuum that makes it effective, but how well the leadership style helps the followers learn and grow. You may use a style that is at the far right of the continuum, but if that is not what the followers need to succeed, it is ineffective. We should strive to develop a leader-follower relationship that operates on the right of the continuum (delegation leadership) realizing that we will often have to use other leadership styles to help our followers progress.

Leadership styles can be compared to a bicycle. The left of the continuum, where leaders are dictatorial, could be compared to training wheels on a bicycle. The right side of the continuum, where leaders give more freedom, could be compared to a 21-speed mountain bike. The follower tries to ride the bike and the leader enables him to ride it. Let's say that the follower is learning how to ride a bike and crashes all the time. An effective leader will place training wheels on the bike for a time until his skills increase and he no longer needs them. An ineffective leader may take an unskilled follower, put him on a mountain bike and just let him go. That leader is setting the follower up for failure. The follower will certainly crash and fail, learning little or nothing and maybe even make him worse than before because of broken bones and feelings of failure.

Another example of an ineffective leader would be one that places training wheels on the bicycle of an experienced and skilled follower. This leadership approach restricts the follower's abilities. With the training wheels on the bike, the follower can't go as fast, or take corners as sharp. The training wheels would restrict the follower from riding the bicycle at his full potential. It is so important that we adapt our leadership style to the abilities and situations of the followers we serve.

The left side of the continuum could also be compared to living by rules and the right side to living by principles. Depending on the spiritual maturity of his children, God has at times given commandments that are rule-based and other times given commandments that are principle-based. As leaders we too have to adjust our leadership style to become more rule-based or principle-based depending on our followers' abilities.

"The commandments of God may be expressed either as rules or as principles, depending on the circumstances of those to whom his word is given. Nevertheless, there is a tremendous difference between rules and principles. Rules are usually based on principles, but rules are "bite sized," specific applications of principles to certain specified situations. Because of their greater specificity, rules are more rigid and inflexible than principles. By design they offer little choice—other than to obey or disobey—and little wiggle room. After all, 'A rule is a rule.' Rules are usually constant; they are the same for every person in every circumstance: 'A rule is a rule.' Because you don't have to understand a rule in order to obey it, rules are a blessing to the young, the inexperienced, or the spiritually immature. The rules automatically apply higher principles for us to many of life's common situations. This they do in a predetermined and almost mechanical manner that does not require much judgment or discernment on the part of those who keep them: 'A rule is a rule.' A prime example of righteousness by rules would be the law of Moses (including the Ten Commandments), which was given to spiritually immature Israel in the wilderness.

"Principles, on the other hand, are not rigid and inflexible in how they are observed, and they may often be appropriately adapted and changed to meet special circumstances, though doing this successfully requires more spiritual maturity and judgment than does merely keeping a rule. This is the great advantage of principle-based righteousness: In order to live our lives by the rules, we would need a rule for every possible human situation, zillions of rules, more than we could ever memorize, but we need only a few principles to live by, and those same few principles can always be appropriately applied to any of life's zillion possible situations. For example, in context of the gospel, the rule against homicide is fulfilled and made obsolete by the principle of love, the rule against adultery by the principle of chastity, and so on. The rules of the law of Moses are good and true, but they are rendered obsolete and unnecessary by living the broader principles of the gospel, which they only partly expressed."[26]

Although for a time we may have to give our followers training wheels or rules to help them succeed, we need to help them progress to a point where they can ride a bike without training wheels and can live by the principles of the gospel. As we help our followers on the ladder toward perfection, there are three main steps. These main divisions are disobedience, obedience to rules, obedience to principles.

Gospel Of Christ: Principal Righteousness; living by principals that apply to all situations.

Law Of Moses: Obey Rules; many rules for each situation, black and white commandments, dos and don'ts.

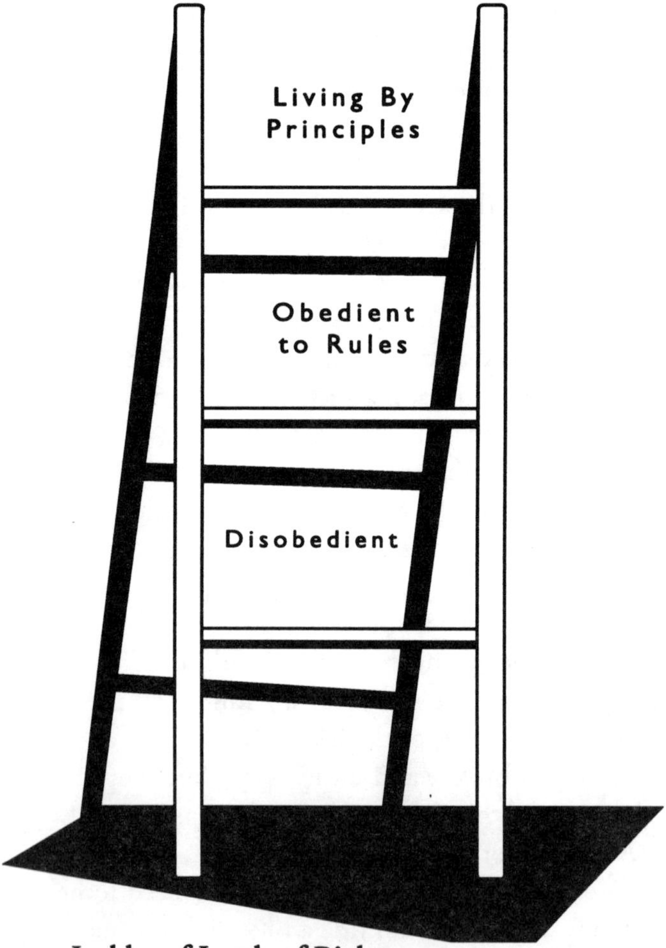

Ladder of Levels of Righteousness

As we help our followers on the ladder toward perfection, there are three main steps: Disobedient, Obedient to Rules and Living by Principles.

We desire to operate on the right side of the continuum (delegation leadership, principle centered, 21-speed mountain bike). However, we shouldn't worry about using rule-based leadership styles if that is what our followers need and it helps them progress. Many times the Lord has used rule-based leadership when needed to help His children progress to a higher level of followership.

For example, the Lord has given us the law of tithing. Tithing is a rule-based law, but it is designed to prepare us for living the principle of consecration. Also, as mentioned earlier, the Lord gave Israel the law of Moses because of their unrighteousness, but He gave them the law to prepare them to live gospel principles. "Wherefore the law was our schoolmaster to bring us unto Christ, that we might be justified by faith. But after that faith is come, we are no longer under a schoolmaster."[27] The law was given to help Israel progress to a higher level of righteousness and live by principles. Once they obtained a higher level of righteousness they were no longer under the schoolmaster. Likewise, when a person learns to ride a bicycle, they take off the training wheels. In fact, if the training wheels are left on after they are no longer needed, they will inhibit the rider's abilities.

We can use rules and training wheels but they should only be temporary. They should be a means of obtaining higher levels of followership. We should strive to cultivate an environment where our followers have the freedom to bring to pass God's work. God encourages us to use our knowledge and creativity to bring forth His work. "Behold, it is not meet that I should command in all things; for he that is compelled in all things, the same is a slothful and not a wise servant; wherefore he receiveth no reward. Verily I say, men should be anxiously engaged in a good cause, and do many things of their own free will, and bring to pass much righteousness; For the power is in them, wherein they are agents unto themselves. And inasmuch as men do good they shall in nowise lose their reward. But he that doeth not anything until he is commanded, and receiveth a commandment with doubtful heart, and keepeth it with slothfulness, the same is damned."[28]

Eventually we will arrive at a leader-follow relationship at the right of the continuum. At this level, the followers operate at what we call self-government. The followers have reached a level of maturity where they are able to act for themselves. Religious leader Joseph Smith's ability to enable his followers to govern themselves was manifested when answering how he was able to lead such a great number of people. Joseph replied, "I teach them correct principles and they govern themselves." How can we lead at a level of self-government? First, both the leader and the follower must be able to operate at that level. Then, the leader-follower relationship operates through what Stephen Covey calls stewardship delegation.

Application Idea for Leadership Styles

1. Strive to live by principles and teach your followers to do the same. Don't be satisfied with living by rules. Often we have heard people say they are only worried about living the rules and if they can follow the letter of the law they are okay. This mentality stagnates their growth. We should not be satisfied with rule-based righteousness, but we should seek to live by the principles of success. Living by rules isn't bad, but we should look for the underlying principles of rules and seek to live by them and also have our followers live by them.

Stewardship Delegation

"Delegating means letting others
become the experts and hence the best."
—Timothy Firnstahl

"Stewardship delegation is focused on results instead of methods. It gives people a choice of methods and makes them responsible for results. It takes more time in the beginning, but it's time well invested. You can move the fulcrum over, you can increase your leverage, through stewardship delegation. Stewardship delegation involves clear, up-front mutual understanding and commitment regarding expectations in five areas:

Desired Results. Create a clear, mutual understanding of what needs to be accomplished, focusing on what, not how; results, not methods. . .

Guidelines. Identify the parameters within which the individual should operate. These should be as few as possible to avoid methods delegation, but should include any formidable restrictions…If you know the failure paths of the job, identify them. Be honest and open—tell a person where the quicksand is and where the wild animals are. You don't want to have to reinvent the wheel every day. Let people learn from your mistakes or the mistakes of others. Point out the potential failure paths, what not to do, but don't tell them what to do. Keep the responsibility for results with them – to do whatever is necessary within the guidelines.

Resources. Identify the human, financial, technical, or organizational resources the person can draw on to accomplish the desired results.

Accountability. Set up standards of performance that will be used in evaluating the results and the specific times when reporting and evaluation will take place.

Consequences. Specify what will happen, both good and bad, as a result of the evaluation. This could include such things as financial rewards, psychic rewards, different job assignments, and natural consequences tied into the overall mission of an organization."[29]

As we use the five elements of stewardship delegation, we help our followers reach their full potential by exerting their creativity and unique talents to obtain the desired results. However, we must only use stewardship delegation when the follower is ready for it. If we use it prematurely it is like placing an inexperienced 7 year old on a 21-speed mountain bike.

Divine-Centered Leaders use the leadership styles that are aligned with the abilities and circumstances of their followers, working toward a leader-follower relationship where the follower operates at his full potential.

Applications Ideas for Stewardship Delegation

1. Think of a stewardship you have and will delegate to someone. Define what each of the five areas of a stewardship delegation—desired results, guidelines, resources, accountability, and consequences—will be for that delegation.

PART 6

Conclusion

PART 6: CONCLUSION

Much of Divine-Centered Leadership can be summed into one word—friendship. There is a close parallel between Christlike leadership and true friendship. Divine-Centered Leaders cultivate strong, loving friendships. Divine-Centered Leaders do not lead as the world leads. They lead others because they love them and want to help them succeed. Divine-Centered Leaders are not the bosses, masters or dictators of others. They are the friends and servants of others. They make sure that other's needs are their highest priority.

Christ was a friend to those he served. Throughout the scriptures, He refers to his followers as friends. In speaking to the New Testament disciples, Jesus said, "Henceforth I call you not servants; for the servant knoweth not what his lord doeth: but I have called you friends; for all things that I have heard of my Father I have made known unto you."[1]

The challenge for Divine-Centered Leaders is to cultivate strong friendships. People follow those they like; they like their friends. Friendships create a willingness to follow.

"You can be a leader without being or having a friend, but you will have chosen the more difficult route. Being a friend is the simpler, easier, more effective way to achieve your goals. Being a friend opens the door to more exciting, moving powerful leadership, without the use of complex, lengthy strategies for winning and influencing others."[2]

The most effective leaders are those who are friends to others. It is not surprising to see children who are more influenced by their friends than by their parents. It is not surprising to see employees who are more influenced by their friends at work than by their bosses. It's not surprising to see church members who are more influenced by their friends than by their leaders. If parents, bosses, and church leaders desire to lead others, they must first cultivate friendships.

We can all describe what a friend does and is, but we often fail to be friends to those we lead. As individuals are given stewardship over another, they often become master instead of servant and friend. "We have learned by sad experience that it is the nature of almost all men, as soon as they get a little authority, as they suppose, they will immediately begin to exercise unrighteous dominion."[3] They become the master of others—controlling, dominating, and dictating—seeking to fulfill their own interests.

The Lord gives us a beautiful rendition of how a friend leads others. "...By persuasion, by long-suffering, by gentleness and meekness, and by love unfeigned; By kindness, and pure knowledge, which shall greatly enlarge the soul without hypocrisy, and without guile—Reproving betimes with sharpness when moved upon by the Holy Ghost; and then showing forth afterwards an increase of love toward him whom thou hast reproved, lest he esteem thee to be his enemy;"[4] Friends love and are servants to their followers. They help others to succeed, invite others to a higher way, inspire and succor. Friends seek to fulfill the needs of others. There is caring and a mutual love between friends.

We know for the most part what a good friend does and is, but how often can we define our leader-follower relationships as that of friends. Often we try to improve our leadership by learning new tactics of influence, or we use new methods of reward and punishment, many of which are needed and helpful. However, we would suggest that if you know how to be a true friend, you know how to be a Christlike leader. Let's begin our quest to be Christlike leaders by being friends to those we lead.

Hopefully, by this point you have come to see the great value of learning and developing Christlike leadership abilities. This book does not contain all the leadership ideas, methods and practices of the Master Jesus Christ. This is just a beginning. We would invite you to continue to study the life of the Savior so you may further understand and emulate His perfect leadership. Utilize the scriptures, other literature, and divine inspiration.

Learning and applying Divine-Centered Leadership is a process. The concepts in this book are not something you learn once. Each concept can be learned and applied on higher and higher levels. You have reached the end of this book, but your journey to live in accordance with the principles of success and to become a Christlike leader continues.

APPENDIX

Developing a Dream Statement *(To obtain the book which contains the complete Statement of Excellence Workshop and further insight and information on the principles of success, call 1- 801-755-5323.)*

This section is designed to help you cultivate vision and define your dreams.

A dream statement helps us clearly define our future desired ends and the direction in which we are going. A dream statement is the process of clearly articulating a dream or vision into writing in such a way that it motivates and inspires us to accomplish that dream. It describes what the future will be like. The key to an effective dream statement is to vividly portrays what we want to accomplish and an ideal state of life. Seek the inspiration of a higher power as you seek to answer the questions that follow. God wants you to accomplish great things. There are things you can do to improve the world which no one else can.

Defining your dream is the most important thing you can do to accomplish great things and to get what you want out of life. Your goals and dreams will give you a definite purpose backed by a burning desire for its fulfillment.

Apathy, laziness, boredom and low self-esteem result from a lack of a dream – from a lack of vision and purpose. As we provide individuals with vision and purpose, we will see new people emerge full of enthusiasm, drive, diligence and dedication to bring forth their dreams. These attributes are within each individual. People simply need a reason to exhibit them. Dreams motivate and create action.

Once you have created a dream statement, you should review it often. You should review it at least twice a day – in the morning when you get up and at night before you go to bed. Visualize what your life will be like when your goals and dreams are achieved. Writing down and visualizing your dreams and goals works. There is great power in writing and reviewing goals. A dream statement enables you to do more for yourself, others, and all the world.

Whatever you can conceive and believe, you can achieve. You will be amazed as your dreams become reality. Faith precedes the miracles. You exercise faith by writing down your dreams and goals, and miracles occur as your goals and dreams come to fruition.

"You owe it to yourself and humanity to set gigantic, seemingly impossible goals that will help everyone. Whether you have high aim or low aim, you will hit it; if you have low aim, you have no aim at all and will hit nothing. It grieves me to watch individuals squander their lives because they have neglected the process of writing down their personal goals. The process of setting and getting goals is fun." (Hansen, Mark Victor, *The Future Diary*, Newport Beach: Mark Victor Hansen Publishing Company, 1996, p. 43)

Books to Assist you in Defining Your Dream

Future Diary by Mark Victor Hansen

Future Diary is a powerful tool to help you see the power of goals and dreams. This book contains powerful text, but it also has several questions and ideas to assist you in writing down your goals and dreams. Mark states in his book, "Pre-determine the objectives you want to accomplish. Think big, act big, and set out to accomplish big results. Big goals turn on the energy in your eighteen billion brain cells. Your vast mind power is waiting to be turned on." Read this book and your mind power will be turned on and you will be on a path to achieving all your goals and dreams.

The Magic of Thinking Big by David J. Schwartz

In building anything—cars, homes, bridges, we need tools. Many people in their attempt to build a successful life forget that there are tools to help them. *The Magic of Thinking Big* is a tool that will help you build your dreams. Much of your success in defining and achieving your dreams will result from how you think. *The Magic of Thinking Big* will develop within you a belief that you can succeed—that anything is possible. *The Magic of Thinking Big* will change the way you think, change the way you act, and fill you with a hope of a better life.

Questions to Help You Define Your Dream:

If I won a million dollars in the lottery what would I do? If I had unlimited time and money, what would I do?

Describe my ideal life? What would I have? What would I do? (Describe specifics)

What vacations would I like to take with my family?

I become like those I associate with. Whom would I like to associate with?

Write the names and characteristics of the people (past and present) I would like to emulate, match, and surpass.

I am my greatest asset. How would I like to grow in these four areas.

Intellectually

What books will I read?

What tapes will I listen to?

What course will I take?

What seminars will I experience?

Physically

What is my desired weight and physical condition?

Socially

What things would I like to do for fun with my family and friends?

Spiritually

What would my faith in Christ be like at my ideal state?

How would I like others to describe me? Whom would I like to become?

Whom would I like to help? What causes would you like to contribute to? What can I do to serve?

How can I make the world a better place?

What would I like to give to family, friends, church, community and the world?

What kind of standard of living do I want to provide for my family? What income level would I like to have? (In 6 months, 1 year, 2 years, 5 years, 10 years, 20 years)

Where would I like to live? Describe my ideal home and surroundings.

What vehicles would I like to own?

What recreational vehicles and toys (boats, motor homes, 4-wheelers, motorcycles, mountain bikes) would I like to own?

What do I deeply enjoy doing?

What recreational activities do I enjoy?

What can I do that would help others?

What do I dream about doing?

List everything I have ever wanted to do, be or have.

What books can I read to help me achieve my dreams? (I would suggest reading *The Cash Flow Quadrant* by Robert T. Kiyosaki plus other books related to your specific dreams.)

Other

____
____
____
____
____
____
____
____
____

Activities to Assist you in Defining Your Dream:

Whatever your dreams are, make them tangible by learning about them. If there is a certain car you would like to have, learn about it, drive it, put pictures of it where you can see them. If you desire a certain vacation, learn about it, get brochures, pictures, and visit web sites about that vacation. If there is a certain group of people or cause you would like to help, find out what help they need and what things they are doing to improve peoples lives. Go look at different houses and neighborhoods to find out what you like and where you may want to live. If you want to be a best-selling author, read books on how to become a best-selling author and talk to people who have done it. If you want to become an artist, read books about it, take classes on it and learn from people who are where you want to be.

Example of a Dream Statement

I have a passive seven-figure income every year allowing me the time and resources to do the things that are truly important. I am debt free and pay cash for everything I do and buy. I donate time and resources to my Church. I associate with some of the greatest men I know: Lennon Ledbetter, Dexter Yager, Stephen Robinson, Stephen Covey, Hyrum Smith, Mark Victor Hansen and many of my Church's leaders.

I own a Steakhouse that is open 24 hours, so I can eat whenever I want with out having to wait. I own a ski boat so I can take my family and friends waterskiing. I have a home with a theater, a full court basketball gym and an exercise room. I have a cabin in the mountains surrounded by trees overlooking a beautiful lake. I also have a home on the island of Lani in Hawaii. I have time everyday to spend with my wife and kids. We spend time as a family doing the things we enjoy—playing sports, serving others, concerts, attending sporting events, eating, and reading. I am a full-time dad and my wife is a full-time mom. I am a hero to each of my children. I never have to work for someone else. I take vacations every year with my family and friends. We have gone to Hawaii, Europe, Australia, Lake Powell, Peter Island, and the Bahamas.

I have several best selling books and I am recognized as one of the most influential writers in history. I have sold over 50 million copies of my various books. I have lectured throughout the world and am considered to be one of the greatest lecturer/teachers ever. I have helped thousands of people achieve their dreams and goals by teaching them the principles of success and introducing them to ways they can achieve their dreams and true happiness.

The best things about my life is that I am free and happy. I have the time and resources to do whatever I believe is worthy of my time. My decisions are based upon what my family and I want to do. They are not dependant on how much time or money we have. My life is filled with love, peace, happiness, integrity, service, and righteousness. I have achieved this life as a result of serving others and keeping the commands of God. I have achieved my dreams, but more importantly I have helped thousands of people achieve their dreams and true joy.

Formulate a Rough Draft of Your Dream Statement (write your dream statement in present and past tense)

____

____

____

____

____

____

____

____

____

Possible Long-Term Goals and Roles

	Role	Role	Role	Role
GOALS				

Possible Short-Term Goals and Roles

GOALS

Role	Role	Role	Role

Possible Short-Term Goals and Roles

ROLE: Personal Development

GOALS

Intellectual	Social	Physical	Spiritual

Short-Term Goal Setting Process / STEPS 4 – 8

STEP 1:Review Statement of Excellence

STEP 2:Set possible short-term goals (Refer to "Possible Short-term Goal Form")

STEP 3:Prioritize possible short-term goals (Refer to Possible "Short-term Goal Form")

Date: Role: Evaluation (day/time):

STEP 4: Weekly Goal

STEP 5: Direction

STEP 6: Benefits

STEP 7: Plan / Schedule Time

STEP 8a: Actual Results

STEP 8b: Evaluation

Balanced Life Evaluation Form

"If a man does not blend into his life a program of self-improvement to bring about a sensible balance, he no doubt will end up a failure."
—John H. Vandenberg

Review how balanced your life is currently and how well you are developing the four aspects of your life by completing the following questions as they relate to you.

Factors	**What level of importance do you place on this factor in evaluating your overall happiness? (0 = being no importance, 10 = being of great importance.)**	**How effective are you in accomplishing your desired results in this area? (0 = low, 10 = High)**
Physical		
Physical Health	0 1 2 3 4 5 6 7 8 9 10	0 1 2 3 4 5 6 7 8 9 10
Exercise	0 1 2 3 4 5 6 7 8 9 10	0 1 2 3 4 5 6 7 8 9 10
Sleeping Habits	0 1 2 3 4 5 6 7 8 9 10	0 1 2 3 4 5 6 7 8 9 10
Eating Habits	0 1 2 3 4 5 6 7 8 9 10	0 1 2 3 4 5 6 7 8 9 10
Financial Well-Being	0 1 2 3 4 5 6 7 8 9 10	0 1 2 3 4 5 6 7 8 9 10
Percentage of Time Spent Per Week Maintaining and Developing the Physical Area of Your Life:		
Social		
Relationship with Self	0 1 2 3 4 5 6 7 8 9 10	0 1 2 3 4 5 6 7 8 9 10
Family Relationships	0 1 2 3 4 5 6 7 8 9 10	0 1 2 3 4 5 6 7 8 9 10
Friends	0 1 2 3 4 5 6 7 8 9 10	0 1 2 3 4 5 6 7 8 9 10
Service	0 1 2 3 4 5 6 7 8 9 10	0 1 2 3 4 5 6 7 8 9 10
Group/Club Relationships	0 1 2 3 4 5 6 7 8 9 10	0 1 2 3 4 5 6 7 8 9 10
Percentage of Time Spent Per Week Maintaining and Developing the Social Area of Your Life:		

Intellectual

Development of Skills and Talents	0 1 2 3 4 5 6 7 8 9 10	0 1 2 3 4 5 6 7 8 9 10
Education	0 1 2 3 4 5 6 7 8 9 10	0 1 2 3 4 5 6 7 8 9 10
Visualization/Planning/Goal Setting	0 1 2 3 4 5 6 7 8 9 10	0 1 2 3 4 5 6 7 8 9 10
Reading	0 1 2 3 4 5 6 7 8 9 10	0 1 2 3 4 5 6 7 8 9 10
Percentage of Time Spent Per Week Maintaining and Developing the Intellectual Area of Your Life:		

Spiritual

Reading Scriptures	0 1 2 3 4 5 6 7 8 9 10	0 1 2 3 4 5 6 7 8 9 10
Prayer/Fasting	0 1 2 3 4 5 6 7 8 9 10	0 1 2 3 4 5 6 7 8 9 10
Spiritual/Church Contributions	0 1 2 3 4 5 6 7 8 9 10	0 1 2 3 4 5 6 7 8 9 10
Meditation	0 1 2 3 4 5 6 7 8 9 10	0 1 2 3 4 5 6 7 8 9 10
Gospel Study	0 1 2 3 4 5 6 7 8 9 10	0 1 2 3 4 5 6 7 8 9 10
Percentage of Time Spent Per Week Maintaining and Developing the Spiritual of Your Life:		

Living a Balanced Life	0 1 2 3 4 5 6 7 8 9 10	0 1 2 3 4 5 6 7 8 9 10

Place a check mark beside the factors that indicate an imbalance between the importance of the item and how effective you are in accomplishing your desired results in that area.

Your time doesn't have to be equally divided between the four areas for there to be a balance but time is required in each area. You need to decide if you are putting the time necessary into each area for you to have a balanced life. Are you putting in the necessary time into each area (spiritual, social, intellectual, physical) or is your life out of balance? What areas do you need to strengthen? How can you improve?

Determine what you can do to ensure your maintenance and development in each aspect of your life (spiritual, intellectual, social, physical).

REFERENCES BY PART

Part 1: Introduction

1. Kimball, Spencer W., "Jesus: The Perfect Leader," *Ensign*, Aug 1979.
2. Maxwell, John C., *Developing the Leader Within You*, (Nashville: Thomas Nelson, Inc., Publishers,) 1993, p. x
3. Tanner, Eldon N., "Leading As the Savior Led," *New Era*, June 1977.
4. Hinckley, Gordon B., "Stand Up for Truth," p. 3
5. Carnegie, Dale, *How to Win Friends and Influence People*, (New York: Pocket Books, 1982), p. xiv.
6. Schartz, David J., *The Magic of Thinking Big*, (New York: Simon and Schuster,) 1959, p. 147

Part 2: The Ladder Model of Divine-Centered Leadership

1. Lewis, C. S., *Mere Christianity*, (London: Harper Collins Publishers Ltd., 1996,) p. 136
2. Kimball, Spencer W., "Jesus: The Perfect Leader," *Ensign*, Aug 1979, p. 5-7
3. John Stott, *Life in Christ*, p.22
4. Doctrine and Covenants 90:5
5. Millet, Robert, *Christ-Centered Living*, (Salt Lake City: Book Craft, 1994), p. 125-126
6. Mere Christianity, London: Harper Collins Publishers Ltd., 1996, p. 191
7. Covey, Stephen, *The Seven Habits of Highly Effective People, (New York: Simon & Schuster)* p. 199
8. Smith, Joseph Fielding, *Teachings of the Prophet Joseph Smith*, (Salt Lake City: Deseret, 1976,) p. 240
9. Hunter, Howard W., "A More Excellent Way," *Ensign*, May 1992.
10. Doctrine and Covenants 121:41
11. Doctrine and Covenants 130: 20-21
12. Lewis, C. S., *Mere Christianity*, p. 69
13. Smith, Hyrum W., *The Ten Natural Laws of Successful Time and Life Management*, (New York: Warner Books, 1994,) p. 147.
14. Packard, Boyd K., *Conference Report*, October 1986, p. 20
15. Covey, Stephen R., *The Seven Habits of Highly Effective People*, (New York: Simon & Schuster,) p. 21

Part 3: Knowing the Way

1. McConkie, Bruce R., *The Promised Messiah*, (Salt Lake City: Deseret, 1982) p. 123
2. Doctrine and Covenants 38:27
3. Matthew 12:30
4. Cannon, George Q., *Gospel Truth*, Vol. 1, p. 210
5. Matthew 12:25
6. Matthew 6:24
7. Harrris, James R., *BYU Studies*, Vol. 8. No. 1, p. 46)
8. Abraham 3:19
9. Maxwell, Neal A., *Men and Women of Christ*, p. 10

10. Sill, Sterling W., *Leadership*, Vol. 1, (Salt Lake City: Bookcraft, 1958) p. 222
11. Ballard, M. Russell, "Strength in Counsel"," *Ensign*, November 1993, p. 77
12. Bennis, Warren and Burt Nanus, *Leaders*, (New York: Harper & Row, 1958), p. 89-90, 93
13. Proverbs 29:18
14. Morrison, Alexander B., *Feed My Sheep*, (Salt Lake City: Desert Book, 1992) p. 83-84
15. Frankl, Viktor E., *Man's Search for Meaning*, in Stephen R. Covey, *First Things First*, (New York: Simon & Schuster, 1994) p. 103
16. Singer, Benjamin, "The Future-Focused Role-Image," in Alvin Toffler, *Learning for Tomorrow: The Role of the Future in Education* (New York: Random House, 1974) p. 19-32, in Stephen R. Covey, *First Things First*, (New York: Simon & Schuster, 1994) p. 103
17. Polak, Fred, *The Image of the Future*, in Stephen R. Covey, *First Things First*, (New York: Simon & Schuster, 1994) p. 103
18. Covey, Stephen R., *First Things First*, (New York: Simon & Schuster, 1994) p. 103-104
19. Hansen, Mark Victor, *The Future Diary, (*Newport Beach: Mark Victor Hansen Publishing Company, 1996,) p. 33-34.
20. Matthew 5:48
21. Moroni 7:6-8
22. Hunter, Howard W., *Conference Report*, April 1967, p. 115
23. Locke, Edwin A., *The Essence of Leadership*, (New York: Lexington Book, 1991) p. 79
24. Covey, Stephen R., *Principle-Centered Leadership*, (New York: Simon & Schuster, 1990) p. 219

Part 4: Going the Way

1. Taylor, Cameron, *The Five Practices of Divine-Centered Leadership*, (Provo: Brigham Young University, 1998,) p. 49-50, 75
2. McConkie, Bruce R., *Mormon Doctrine*, p. 26
3. *Gospel Principles*, (Salt Lake City: The Church of Jesus Christ of Latter-day Saints, 1995) p. 23
4. Smith, Joseph Fielding, Jr., *The Way to Perfection*, p. 181
5. Lewis, C. S., *Mere Christianity*, (New York: Simon & Schuster, 1996) p. 87
6. Covey, Stephen R., *The Seven Habits of Highly Effective People*, (New York: Simon and Schuster, 1989) p. 72-73
7. Luke 23:34
8. Hebrews 4:15
9. Brinley, Douglas E., *Strengthening Your Marriage and Family*, (Salt Lake City: Bookcraft, 1994) p. 53, 163-16
10. Kouzes, James M., Barry Z. Posner, *The Leadership Challenge*, (San Francisco: Jossey-Bass, 1995) p. 36
11. Maxwell, Neal A., *A More Excellent Way*, p.34
12. Fluckinger, Lynn, *Dynamic Leadership*, (Salt Lake City: Desert Book, 1962) p. 50
13. 2 Nephi 28:24-29
14. Revelations 3:15-16
15. Matthew 25:21
16. Matthew 25:26-27, 30
17. *Teachings of the Prophet Joseph Smith*, Section Six 1843–44, p.348
18. *Teachings of the Prophet Joseph Smith*, Section Six 1843–44, p. 51
19. Cox, James B., *How to Qualify for the Celestial Kingdom Today*, (Riverton, Utah: Ensign, 1984) p. 37

20. Doctrine and Covenants 93:12-13
21. 3 Nephi 11:29
22. Tjosvold, Dean, *Learning to Manage Conflict*, (New York: Lexington Book, 1993) p. 4-5
23. Mayer, Richard J., *Conflict Management*, (Columbus: Battelle, 1990) p. 81, 85, 86
24. McKay, David O., *Personal Radiation*, BYU April 27, 1948
25. Maxwell, John C., *Developing the Leader Within You*, (Nashville: Thomas Nelson, Inc., Publishers, 1993,) p. 132
26. Millet, Robert L., *The Challenge of Christ-Centered Leadership*, Address given to Wright Leadership Seminar March 16, 1992)
27. 3 Nephi 19:9
28. 3 Nephi 19:9
29. "Guidance of the Holy Spirit," *Ensign*, January, 1980, p. 5
30. Job 27:5-6
31. John 17:13
32. Mosiah 3:19
33. Robinson, Stephen E., *Following Christ*, p. 56-57
34. *The Teachings of Spencer W. Kimball*, p.198
35. Covey, Stephen R, *First Things First*, (New York: Simon & Schuster, 1994) p. 175, 178
36. Matthew 16:26
37. Kimball, Spencer W., *Faith Precedes the Miracle*, p. 236, 238
38. Kimball, Spencer W., *Faith Proceeds the Miracle*, p. 244
39. *BYU Speeches*, December 12, 1962, p.2
40. Lewis, C. S., *Mere Christianity*, (New York: Simon & Schuster, 1980) p.87
41. Luke 2:52
42. Doctrine and Covenants 29:34
43. Young, Brigham, *Discourses of Brigham Young*, p.238 - p.239

Part 5: Showing the Way

1. Taylor, Cameron, *The Five Practices of Divine-Centered Leadership*, (Provo: Brigham Young University, 1998,) p. 100
2. Taylor, Cameron, *The Five Practices of Divine-Centered Leadership*, (Provo: Brigham Young University, 1998,) p. 125
3. Lewis, C. S., Mere Christianity, (New York: Simon & Schuster, 1996) p. 176
4. Sill, Sterling W., *Leadership*, vol. 3, (Salt Lake City: Bookcraft, 1978) p. 59
5. Sill, Sterling W., *Leadership*, vol. 3, (Salt Lake City: Bookcraft, 1978) p. 60
6. Lewis, C. S., *The Weight of Glory*, (New York: Simon & Schuster, 1996) p. 39
7. Covey, Stephen R., *The Divine-Center*, (Salt Lake City: Bookcraft, 1982) p. 165-66
8. Roberts, B. H., *The Seventy's Course in Theology*, Fifth Year, p. 46-7
9. Covey, Stephen R., *The Seven Habits of Highly Effective People,* (New York: Simon & Schuster, 1989) p. 277-278
10. Doctrine and Covenants. 84:109-110
11. Covey, Stephen R., *The Seven Habits of Highly Effective People*, (New York: Simon & Schuster, 1989) p. 284
12. Carnegie, Dale, *How to Win Friends and Influence People*, (New York: Pocket Books, 1982,) p. 75-83
13. Covey, Stephen R., *How to Succeed with People*, (Salt Lake City: Deseret Book, 1971) p. 51- 53

14. Covey, Stephen R., *The Seven Habits of Highly Effective People*, (New York: Simon & Schuster, 1989) p.193-4
15. Matthew 7:12
16. Skinner, Rulon, *Twenty-two Leadership Principles*, (BYU: 1979) p. 188
17. Skinner, Rulon, *Twenty-two Leadership Principles*, (BYU: 1979) p. 188
18. Skinner, Rulon, *Twenty-two Leadership Principles*, (BYU: 1979) p. 188
19. Skinner, Rulon, *Twenty-two Leadership Principles*, (BYU: 1979) p. 188
20. Fischer, Louis, *The Essential Gandhi*, (New York: Random House, 1962) p. 255
21. Greenleaf, Robert, *Servant Leadership*, (New York: Paulist, 1977) p. 13-14
22. Doctrine and Covenants 51:19
23. Doctrine and Covenants 72:3-4, 51:19
24. *Ensign*, Nov. 1980 p. 93
25. *Ensign*, Nov. 1978 p. 81
26. Robinson, Stephen E., *Following Christ*, p. 129-130
27. Galatians 3:24-25
28. Doctrine and Covenants 58:26-2
29. Covey, Stephen, *Seven Habits of Highly Effective People*, (New York: Simon & Schuster, 1989) p. 173-74

Part 6: Conclusion

1. John 15:15
2. Mills, Gordon, *Organizational Behavior* 347 *Course Syllabus*, p. 49
3. Doctrine and Covenants 121:39
4. Doctrine and Covenants 121:41-43

REFERENCES ALPHABETICAL BY AUTHOR

Ashton, Marvin J., *Ensign*, May 1978, p. 8.
Ballard, M. Russell, "Strength in Counsel"," Ensign, November 1993, p. 77.
Bennis, Warren and Burt Nanus, *Leaders*, New York: Harper & Row, 1958.
Benson, Ezra Taft, "Seek the Spirit of the Lord," *Ensign,* April 1988.
Brinley, Douglas E., *Strengthening Your Marriage and Family,* Salt Lake City: Bookcraft, 1994.
Brigham Young University Student Leadership Seminar Curriculum,1998.
Cannon, George Q., *Gospel Truth,* Vol. 1, Salt Lake City: Desert,1987.
Carnegie, Dale, *How to Win Friends and Influence People*, New York: Pocket Books, 1982.
Clark, J. Richard, *Ensign*, Nov. 1978 p.81.
Condie, Spencer J., *Ensign*, May 1990, p. 27.
Covey, Stephen R., *First Things First*, New York: Simon &Schuster, 1994.
Covey, Stephen R., *How to Succeed with People*, Salt Lake City:Deseret Book, 1971.
Covey, Stephen R., *Principle-Centered Leadership*, New York:Simon & Schuster, 1990.
Covey, Stephen R., *The Divine-Center*, Salt Lake City: Bookcraft,1982.
Covey, Stephen R., *The Seven Habits of Highly Effective People*, New York: Simon & Schuster, 1989.
Cox, James B., "How to Qualify for the Celestial Kingdom Today, Riverton," Utah: *Ensign*, 1984.
Derrick Royden G., *Ensign*, May 1977, p. 14.
Evans, Joy R., *Ensign*, May 1989, p. 75.
Fischer, Louis, *The Essential Gandhi*, New York: Random House,1962.
Fluckinger, Lynn, *Dynamic Leadership*, Salt Lake City: Desert Book,1962.
Frankl, Viktor E., *Man's Search for Meaning*, New York: Pocket Books, 1959.
Gardner, Quinn R., *Address, Missionary Training Center*, Provo, Utah, March 1980.
Gospel Principles, Salt Lake City: The Church of Jesus Christ of Latter-day Saints, 1995.
Greenleaf, Robert, *Servant Leadership*, New York: Paulist, 1977.
Haight, David B., *Ensign*, May 1981, p. 42.
Hales, Robert D., *Ensign*, May 1987, p. 75.
Hansen, Mark Victor, *Future Diary*, Newport Beach: Mark Victor Hansen Publishing Company, 1996.
Harrris, James R., *BYU Studies*, Vol. 8. No. 1.
Hinckley, Gordon B., "Stand Up for Truth," *BYU Address*, September 17, 1996.
Hunter, Howard W., *Conference Report*, April 1967.
Hunter, Howard W., *Ensign*, "A More Excellent Way," May 1992.
Hunter, Howard W., *BYU Speeches*, December 12, 1962, p.2.
Kimball, Spencer W., *Faith Precedes the Miracle*, Salt Lake City: Deseret Book,1972.
Kimball, Spencer W., "Jesus: The Perfect Leader," *Ensign*, Aug 1979.
Kimball, Spencer W., *Regional Representatives Seminar*, April 3, 1974.
Kimball, Spencer, *The Teachings of Spencer W. Kimball*, Salt Lake City: Bookcraft, 1991.
Kimball, Spencer W., *Ensign*, March 1976, p. 4.
Kouzes, James M., Barry Z. Posner, *The Leadership Challenge*, San Francisco: Jossey-Bass, 1995.
Lewis, C. S., *Mere Christianity*, London: Harper Collins Publishers Ltd., 1996.
Lewis, C. S., *The Weight of Glory*, New York: Simon & Schuster, 1996.
Locke, Edwin A., *The Essence of Leadership*, New York: Lexington Book, 1991.

Maxwell, John C., *Developing the Leader Within You,* Nashville: Thomas Nelson, Inc., Publishers, 1993.
Maxwell, Neal A., *A More Excellent Way*, Salt Lake City: Deseret Book, 1969.
Maxwell, Neal A., *Men and Women of Christ*, Salt Lake City: Deseret Book, 1991.
Mayer, Richard J., *Conflict Management*, Columbus: Battelle, 1990.
McConkie, Bruce R., *The Promised Messiah*, Salt Lake City: Deseret, 1982.
McConkie, Bruce R., *Millennial Messiah*, Salt Lake City: Deseret, 1982.
McConkie, Bruce R., *Mormon Doctrine*, Salt Lake City: Bookcraft, 1966.
McKay, David O., *Personal Radiation,* Address, BYU, April 27, 1948.
Merrill, Roger, "Followership: Nay, but I Will Be Thy Servant."
Millet, Robert, *Christ-Centered Living*, Salt Lake City: Book Craft, 1994.
Morrison, Alexander B., *Feed My Sheep*, Salt Lake City: Desert Book, 1992.
Nanus, Burt, *Visionary Leadership*, San Francisco: Jossey-Bass Inc., 1992.
Pakard, Boyd K., *Conference Report* 1996, p. 20.
Polak, Fred, *The Image of the Future*, San Francisco: Jossey-Bass, 1972.
Rassmussen, Dennis, "I Know My Sheep."
Roberts, B. H., *The Seventy's Course in Theology*, Fifth Year, Salt Lake City: Deseret News, 1912.
Robinson, Stephen E., *Following Christ*, Salt Lake City: Deseret Book, 1995.
Romney, Marion G., *Ensign*, Nov. 1980 p.93.
Romney, Marion G., "Guidance of the Holy Spirit," *Ensign*, January, 1980, p.5
Schartz, David J., *The Magic of Thinking Big*, New York: Simon and Schuster, 1959.
Scott, Richard G., "Do What is Right," *BYU Address*, March 3, 1996.
Sill, Sterling W., *Leadership*, Vol. 1, Salt Lake City: Bookcraft, 1958.
Sill, Sterling W., *Leadership*, Vol. 3, Salt Lake City: Bookcraft, 1978.
Singer, Benjamin, "The Future-Focused Role-Image," in Alvin Toffler, *Learning for Tomorrow: The Role of the Future in Education*, New York: Random House, 1974.
Skinner, Rulon, *Twenty-Two Leadership Principles*, BYU, 1979.
Smith, Hyrum W., *The Ten Natural Laws of Successful Time and Life Management*, New York: Warner Books, 1994.
Smith, Joseph F., *Improvement Era*, 6:501.
Smith, Joseph Fielding, *Church History and Modern Revelation*, Vol 1.
Smith, Joseph Fielding, *Teachings of the Prophet Joseph Smith*, Salt Lake City: Deseret, 1976.
Smith, Joseph Fielding, *The Way to Perfection*, Salt Lake City: Deseret Book, 1984.
Snow, Lorenzo, *Teachings of Lorenzo Snow*, Salt Lake City: Bookcraft, 1996.
Stepsis, Joan A., *Conflict-Resolutions Strategies.*
Tanner, Eldon N., "Leading As the Savior Led", *New Era*, June 1977.
Taylor, Cameron, *The Five Practices of Divine-Centered Leadership,* Provo: Brigham Young University, 1998.
Tjosvold, Dean, *Learning to Manage Conflict,* New York: Lexington Book, 1993.
Vandenberg, John H., *Conference Report*, October 1972, p. 26.
Young, Brigham, *Discourses of Brigham Young,* Salt Lake City: Deseret Book, 1954.